WORKPLACE DRUG ABUSE AND AIDS

WORKPLACE DRUG ABUSE AND AIDS

A Guide to Human Resource Management Policy and Practice

Donald Klingner with Nancy G. O'Neill

QUORUM BOOKS

NEW YORK • WESTPORT, CONNECTICUT • LONDON

Library of Congress Cataloging-in-Publication Data

Klingner, Donald E.
Workplace drug abuse and AIDS : a guide to human resource
management policy and practice / Donald Klingner with Nancy G.
O'Neill.
p.   cm.
Includes index.
ISBN 0-89930-624-1 (alk. paper)
1. Drugs and employment—United States. 2. Drug testing—United
States. 3. AIDS (Disease)—United States—Diagnosis. 4. Employee
assistance programs—United States. I. O'Neill, Nancy G.
II. Title.
HF5549.5.D7K55   1991
658.3 ' 82—dc20   90-46719

British Library Cataloguing in Publication Data is available.

Library of Congress Catalog Card Number: 90-46719
ISBN: 0-89930-624-1

First published in 1991

Quorum Books, 88 Post Road West, Westport, CT 06881
An imprint of Greenwood Publishing Group, Inc.

Printed in the United States of America

The paper used in this book complies with the
Permanent Paper Standard issued by the National
Information Standards Organization (Z39.48-1984).

10 9 8 7 6 5 4 3 2 1

Copyright Acknowledgment

The author and publisher wish to acknowledge Betsy Freeman of the
Greater Miami Chamber of Commerce for permission to reprint extracts
from "Business Against Drugs" as Appendix A in this volume.

Contents

Tables

Preface

Writing a book is a bit like raising a child. It begins as a gleam in your eye. You form it, shape it, and watch it take on a life of its own. And once it becomes mature it passes into the publisher's hands, beyond your control entirely. You can only hope you have done enough and that it may be well received as it makes its way into the world.

There remains the obligation to write well, and creatively. A book is like a child in that the need to create causes both a sense of joy and a sense of responsibility— joy when things come together with clarity, and responsibility for approaching complex subjects with clarity and insight. So much has been written on substance abuse and AIDS that it is better to say nothing at all than to say nothing new. And so this book is dedicated to those employees, human resource managers, and researchers who have spurred me to write, and to whom the book is dedicated: Alvah Chapman, Marilyn Culp, Robert Denhardt, J. Malcolm Moore, Faustino Pino, M. Gamal Sabet, Ray Surette, and Sally Williams. I can only hope that it does justice to the insights they gave me and the dilemmas they defined.

Nancy G. O'Neill deserves special thanks for her review of the entire manuscript, and particularly her assistance in writing chapters 2 and 8. She opened my eyes to the close relationship between drug and AIDS testing and national health care policy issues. For this I am grateful.

Ralph O'Fallon checked all the footnote citations for accuracy and completeness. Naturally, any remaining errors of fact or omission are my own.

John Hughes of Carolina Academic Press turned the manuscript into a finished book.

Lastly, I wish to thank Cesar Antonio Garcia for raising the question which hindsight now reveals to have sparked my immediate involvement with this topic. Three years ago on a hillside in Ecuador, he asked me, "Why do Americans take so many drugs?"—demonstrating once again that you have to ask the right questions before you can hope to find the right answers.

Introduction

PROBLEMS AND DILEMMAS

The fascinating thing about human resource management is that it always presents the observant researcher or personnel manager with new problems and dilemmas. The problems are inevitably of the "how to" variety—they arise out of managerial needs within the agency or company. One example might be how to develop orientation programs for new employees which emphasize the increased role of safety and health in managing risk or reducing health care costs. Another is how to use assessment center techniques and psychological stress evaluations to reduce the number of police officers who "wash out" while in the training academy or during their probationary period.

But the dilemmas are different—they have no solutions! Instead, they require the human resource management professional to carefully consider conflicting values and objectives and to develop employer policies and practices which manage to recognize and reconcile these conflicts. As always, the value conflicts sharpen these dilemmas. Private sector employers are primarily responsible for maximizing efficiency, as measured by profit or return on investment. But like public sector employers, law and the public interest also make them responsible for achieving other contradictory objectives—political responsiveness, individual rights, and social equity. Inevitably, the solutions that work best to protect the interests of one group work most strongly against the interests of others. Drugs and AIDS are two clear examples of these conflicts.

SUBSTANCE ABUSE AND AIDS

The issue of substance abuse testing has arisen in the last five years because employers are increasingly aware of how much substance abuse costs—not only in lost productivity, but also through increased health care costs and liability risks. And the federal government has contributed to this awareness by increasingly viewing the workplace as a battleground in the "war on drugs." Yet substance testing programs themselves are degrading and invasive, a throwback to the manipulative and primitive practices which characterized personnel management in the days before the Hawthorne experiments and human relations theory established the value of employee understanding and commitment to organizational productivity. And the workplace controversy between efficiency and employee rights is taking place within the context of a more general societal dilemma concerning substance abuse within the larger population and appropriate public policy responses to it.

And as if one dilemma were not enough, human resource managers have a second—AIDS. While this issue affects a smaller number of employees, the value conflicts it invokes are more explosive than those focusing around substance abuse, from every perspective. Take costs. AIDS is invariably fatal, attacks employees at a young and productive age, and results in medical costs ranging from $100,000 to $250,000 from onset to death. The invariable response of insurance carriers or employers who elect to self-insure is to "cap" their health benefit costs. They do this by seriously considering testing all applicants for the AIDS virus antibodies—despite the dubious legality of this strategy—and either refusing to hire those who test positive or excluding them from health benefits coverage for preexisting conditions. Yet this solution is ineffective because of the lengthy incubation period for the virus. It is also repugnant to most personnel managers who recognize the legitimacy of individual rights (particularly the privacy of employees' personal lives and the confidentiality of their medical records). And it is really no solution at all. Rather, it only raises still tougher dilemmas. Under what conditions, if any, are employers justified in basing selection and promotion decisions on a blood test? Given the moral and social stigma attached to AIDS victims, how is it possible to maintain privacy and confidentiality for employees and applicants who test positive for the AIDS virus? Co-workers and union leaders panic and demand that employees with AIDS be isolated or discharged. How can personnel directors develop employee orientation programs and personnel policies that respond to these demands while at the same time protect the dignity and employment rights of those who are infected with AIDS but are still productive employees?

Substance abuse and AIDS may require us to confront the ultimate personnel management dilemma—the implicit creation of a "two-tier" labor market by the personnel policy decisions of individual employers.

THE IMPACT OF SUBSTANCE ABUSE AND AIDS ON PERSONNEL SYSTEMS

One dominant characteristic of public- and private-sector employment has been the increase in benefit costs as a percentage of total payroll. Since 1960, benefits (primarily life insurance and health care) have increased from about 10 percent of payroll to 40 percent–45 percent, in both the public and private sectors.

The reasons for this are readily apparent. First, employers have generally come to recognize that benefits are a necessary condition of employment. A competitive benefits package is necessary to attract and retain high-quality workers. Second, the cost of health care benefits has risen so dramatically that group insurance policies are the only ones affordable by most people. Currently, about 37 percent of all persons in the United States are without any health care insurance whatsoever. Third, changing values and tough competition for tax dollars have reduced the availability of public funds for social services, including health care. The result of these trends is that employers have found themselves increasingly responsible for administering health care programs for their employees and assuming the costs of these programs.

Substance abuse has dramatically affected employers during the past decade. AIDS will be the personnel issue of the 1990s. Taken together, they will have tremendous impact on productivity, health care costs, and liability risks.

Substance abuse increases health care costs because the problem is widespread (about 10 percent of the work force); expensive to treat (inpatient treatment services frequently cost $20,000–$30,000 per month); and not often successful. (While claims of successful treatment regimens abound among health care providers, success rates of about 10 percent to 15 percent are the highest that can be validated by independent sources after a five-year period.) Substance abuse is a liability risk because substance abusers are more likely to engage in behaviors which place the employer (or customers, clients, and employees) at risk. And once an employer has reasonable cause to know that an employee is a substance abuser, the employer assumes civil liability (42 U.S.C. 1983) for the employee's actions on the job.

AIDS is also a health care cost and a liability risk. The disease is invariably fatal. Between onset and death, total health care costs are estimated at $100,000–$250,000 per patient. These are crippling costs for life and health insurance carriers because they are heavy and they occur at an age (35–50) at which employees are usually healthy.

Life and health insurance carriers have responded to substance abuse and AIDS by seeking to minimize their own risks and payouts. This has meant rejecting employees' claims for costs of treatment resulting from conditions existing prior to coverage, reducing contractual benefits, or increasing contractual costs of health care plans. They have often attempted to reject applications for life or health insurance from persons in high-risk groups (regardless of whether those persons' individual medical history or behavior places them at greater risk of being substance abusers or AIDS carriers).

But efforts by insurance carriers or employers to reduce health care costs and liability risks surreptitiously by rejecting applicants who are substance abusers or who test positive for AIDS are also illegal. The existence of these practices, whether as part of a formal policy or informal practice, is a violation of laws regulating insurance companies. It is also a violation of civil rights laws protecting the employment rights of handicapped persons. The development of "blacklists" is a violation of the liberty interest of public employees.

Thus, it is reasonable to conclude that substance abuse and AIDS have confronted personnel systems with the threat of reduced productivity, increased liability risks, and increased health care costs. While productivity and liability risks can be managed, increased health care costs cannot. The costs are too great to be borne by the employee, the employer, or the health insurance carrier. To screen out AIDS carriers is both technically difficult and legally perilous, although it is apparently the most rational solution for personnel managers to adopt.

THE DEVELOPMENT OF A TWO-TIER LABOR MARKET AS A RATIONAL RESPONSE BY EMPLOYERS

The next appropriate solution employers are adopting is the development of a two-tier labor market. Under this system, all current employees (particularly those in managerial and professional positions) are included in a preferential "first-tier" labor market. They are provided with health and life insurance benefits and pensions. If they develop substance abuse problems, these are treated to the extent available under the employer's health insurance. If they test positive for the AIDS virus, they receive the medical benefits to which they are entitled, and their heirs receive life insurance benefits (because these conditions presumably did not predate their employment).

Increasingly, employees in other job categories are hired through an alternative "second-tier" labor market. The distinguishing characteristics of this labor market are that it provides fewer (if any) benefits, and results in lower (if any) liability risks for the employer. Its most common variants are contracting out, leased employees, part-time or seasonal employees, and temporary employees.

Contracting out occurs with increasing frequency in both the public and private sectors. The contractor agrees to perform a specified service for a specified price. This includes all (if any) employee benefits. The contractor assumes liability risks for its employees.

The number of leased employees has tripled in the past four years. Under these arrangements, the employer leases an employee from an agency, which again is responsible for that employee's benefits and liability risks under a performance contract.

Temporary, part-time, and seasonal employees normally have fewer rights than full-time employees. If there is a union, they may be excluded from a collective bargaining agreement. They may be excluded from coverage by the employer's pension, health benefits, or life insurance systems. They may usually be hired and fired at will, without just cause or due process. Employees in these types of positions therefore have fewer benefits than their full-time, permanent counterparts. And the benefits and liability risks can usually be terminated more easily by the employer.

The process by which a two-tier labor market emerges is systemic. The employer can decide to contract out (and release permanent employees who had been performing the function). The employer can sign a collective bargaining agreement under which new employees are hired in at lower pay and benefits than are current employees. Or the employer can simply require that all employees who wish to be considered for first-tier positions be able to pass a substance abuse test and a blood test for the AIDS virus. Those employees who fail either test are simply not considered for permanent, full-time employment.

CONSEQUENCES

This trend has some consequences for our individual rights, for our society, and for our political system.

The trend toward a two-tier labor market requires applicants and employees to confront the consequences of their behavior on their employability in the first-tier labor market. But substance abuse and AIDS are not entirely the result of an individual's choices. To assume that they are, and to establish consequences accordingly, brings any discussion of the causes of these problems to a close. An equally important issue is whether job applicants can reasonably be expected to waive their rights to privacy by voluntarily consenting to the use of a blood test or urinalysis as a condition of employment in the first-tier labor market. Do persons have the right to voluntarily waive constitutional rights, even if it may benefit them to do so?

It obviously makes sense for employers to attempt to reduce their liability risks by screening out applicants who are substance abusers or who test positive for AIDS. However, the relegation of these persons to a second-tier labor market means that the costs of treating (or not treating) their substance abuse and AIDS are simply externalized to the broader environment—society as a whole.

In the long run, this strategy will not be effective because it is based on two fallacious assumptions. First, externalizing the costs of AIDS from first-tier employers to society will not be effective. Because society does not have the resources to deal with these public health problems, their costs tend to revert back to first-tier employers and their employees, who presumably have the resources to address them. Second, substance abuse and AIDS testing will not succeed in keeping these problems from spreading to the work force of first-tier employees. Because these problems are societal, they tend to spread from society to first-tier employers and their employees.

Finally, the creation of a two-tier labor market is a politically ominous development. Access to jobs is the most powerful means that individuals and groups have of attaining or maintaining social, economic, and political status. The demographics of both substance abuse and AIDS guarantees that the groups most likely to be excluded from the first-tier labor market are those already the most dispossessed—urban minorities, intravenous drug users, and male homosexuals. The costs of substance abuse and AIDS are borne by the rest of society if the individual cannot afford them, through either the public health system or the criminal justice system. Adopting a strategy of denial through benign neglect of substance abusers and AIDS carriers will not work, because both problems will inexorably spread into the general population. And a containment strategy based on increased law enforcement and incarceration will be counterproductive because prisons have proven to be a breeding ground for both substance abuse and AIDS, first concentrating together substance abusers and AIDS carriers in an environment where both problems are likely to increase, and then releasing them into society. The economic and political consequences of requiring employers and insurance carriers to continue to carry the burden of substance abuse and AIDS are unbearable. But so are the political, social, and economic consequences of adopting implicit national human resource policies which contribute further to the marginalization of these already disadvantaged groups.

This book will address substance abuse and AIDS in the workplace. It will consider them together, because together they constitute the toughest challenges to professional management of human resources in this century. I hope that the information this book presents and the ideas it raises will be of use to my fellow personnel professionals in addressing these dilemmas.

Part I
Substance Abuse Testing

Substance Abuse in the Workplace

Drug and alcohol abuse is a tremendous problem in our society, from a legal, economic, social, political, and managerial perspective. Media coverage has focused primarily on illegal drugs such as marijuana, cocaine, and "crack." Yet the most widely used drugs, and those representing the greatest health and safety hazard to employees, are alcohol and tobacco.

The most recent National Institute on Drug Abuse (NIDA) survey reports that about 60 percent of the population has used alcohol within the last 30 days, and that about 32 percent use tobacco.[1] The U.S. government reports that over 60 million Americans have tried marijuana, and approximately 20 million have used cocaine. Nearly 23 million individuals can be classified as current users of marijuana (use within the last thirty days), and at least 5 million as current cocaine users. In the 18–25-year-old young adult population representing those entering the work force, 65 percent have experience with illicit drugs, 44 percent within the last year.[2] In the military, before mass drug testing was instituted, 27 percent of twenty-thousand recruits admitted that they had used drugs within the previous 30 days.[3]

It is clear that these drugs are enormous public health problems. It is also clear that (with the exception of tobacco) they can substantially alter human behavior, including the range of skills and abilities necessary for both job behavior and day-to-day functioning in our society. For example, alcohol, marijuana, and prescription tranquilizers or barbiturates affect the ability to drive a car or operate machinery. Alcohol and cocaine may lead to emotional changes, such as irritability or anger. Yet the prevalence of the problem and its effects on employees in the workplace are hard to describe adequately and completely. In addition, it is hard to separate the impact of alcohol and other drugs from the broader effects of workplace conditions, employee skill deficiencies, personality problems, and personal pressures. Many employees who have a problem with drugs or alcohol are using these in an attempt to reduce stress caused by problems in relationships, boredom, depression, etc.

OBJECTIVES

The purpose of this chapter is to:

1. Review the problem of alcohol and other drugs in our society, from social, economic, legal, and political perspectives.

2. Review the range of solutions currently being considered or used to address this problem at a societal level.

3. Examine the impact of workplace alcohol and drug abuse on employers from lost productivity, increased liability risks, and increased health care costs.

4. Introduce the general strategies employers have used to combat this problem: development of policies on alcohol and drug abuse, testing of applicants and employees, and development of employee assistance programs (EAPs) for treating employees with substance abuse problems.

SUBSTANCE ABUSE—AN AMERICAN PROBLEM

While it is easy to assume that drug abuse is restricted to illegal drugs, this book will focus on alcohol as well, for public health experts widely acknowledge that alcohol abuse is the largest drug problem in our society. In addition, experts recognize that alcohol and drug abusers are not two groups of people, but one. Alcoholics cannot safely use drugs, and drug addicts cannot safely use alcohol. Moreover, treatment centers have reported for at least ten years that a majority of patients under the age of forty are dually addicted to alcohol and at least one other drug.[4] Therefore, the general term "substance abuse" will be used interchangeably with "alcohol and drug abuse," for they are the same thing.

Table 1
Lifetime, Annual, and Thirty-Day Drug Use in the United States

	Lifetime	12 Month	30 Days
Alcohol	86.1%	78.6%	59.2%
Tobacco	75.7	36.3	31.5
Tranquilizers	8.9	3.5	1.1
Marijuana	32.5	15.3	9.4
Inhalants	6.8	1.5	.9
Steroids	1.1	.4	.4
Cocaine	15.4	6.3	2.9
LSD	3.7	0.0	0.0
Psychedelics	6.7	1.4	*
Amphetamines	9.2	4.1	1.3
Barbiturates	6.0	2.6	.8
Crack	1.3	.4	0.0
Heroin	.2	0.0	0.0

Since 1971, NIDA has sponsored a series of National Household Surveys to measure the prevalence of drug use among the American household population aged twelve and over. These data were collected by selecting a random sample of Americans, stratified by important demographic variables (age, sex, race/ethnicity, and region of the country) and weighted to reflect the characteristics of the national population as a whole in 1985. All of the findings given in Table 1 are taken from the 1988 report, the most recent for which published data are available.[5] It is important to remember that the Household Survey data are self-reported; that is, the incidence of use of a particular drug is likely to be higher than reported for illegal drugs.

The NIDA Household Survey asked Americans if they had experienced problems as a result of their alcohol or drug use. The most common problem was with unclear thinking—between 7.1 percent and 11.9 percent found it difficult to think clearly because of their alcohol or drug use. Other problems most often experienced in the past year were arguments with family or friends (6.7 percent), unsafe driving (7.4 percent), depression (5.8 percent), loss of memory of events that occurred while drunk or high (5.8 percent), and anxiety (5.6 percent).[6]

It is also important to understand that in most cases there is a direct relationship between the extent of substance abuse and the extent of personal problems resulting from substance abuse. For example, about 85 percent of those who smoke more than a pack of cigarettes per day have tried to cut down. Forty-nine percent of those who reported being drunk more than twice a month said they were aggressive while drinking; 41 percent reported heated arguments while drinking, and 54 percent reported they were unable to remember what happened while they were drinking. Generally, those respondents who reported drinking problems were in the 12–34-year-old age group.

These patterns were also repeated for illegal drugs. Again, there is a direct relationship between the extent of substance abuse and the extent of personal problems resulting from substance abuse, and those respondents who report drug problems are likely to be in the 12–34-year-age group. Again, we must remember that the incidence of problems is likely to be lower than it is in reality because it is self-reported.

DRUG ABUSE IS A PROBLEM FOR AMERICAN SOCIETY

A Gallup poll conducted in the summer of 1989 reported that, for the first time since the end of World War II, a majority of Americans considered a domestic issue to be the most important one facing the United States today. The issue? Drug abuse. A corroborating poll conducted at the same time by the *Wall Street Journal* and NBC indicated that 43 percent consider drugs to be the nation's single most important issue; the next most frequently cited concern, the budget deficit, was named by only 6 percent.[7] And the reasons for this choice are clear: Substance abuse is not only a problem for individual Americans, it is a societal problem with economic, social, legal, and political impacts.

First, substance abuse is an *economic* issue. According to the latest federal government estimates, 12 percent of the American work force of 114 million persons (13.5 million) have alcohol problems. Of the $117 billion loss due to alcohol in 1983, $70 billion resulted from reduced work productivity and lost employment. Alcohol abuse will cost the economy $130 billion a year by the end of 1990.[8]

As a *social* issue, substance abuse causes or worsens a range of other problems, including infant mortality, crime, and educational dropouts. The infant mortality rate in the District of Columbia in 1989 was 27 per 1,000, nearly three times the national rate. A black infant born in the District of Columbia is more likely to die before the age of one than a baby born in North Korea or Bulgaria. Experts explain the high mortality rate by stating that 60–70 percent of the babies are born to women who used drugs or alcohol while pregnant, or who did not take advantage of available prenatal care programs.[9]

Substance abuse is a *legal* issue because the possession of many drugs for sale or personal use is illegal under federal and state law. Therefore, law enforcement officials agree that drugs are responsible for a significant part of the increased crime rate. For minority youth who lack education and jobs, the opportunity to earn big money selling drugs is a powerful incentive in our individualistic and capitalistic society. And for those who buy, the cost of drugs is often met by purse snatchings and residential burglaries. Experts estimate that about 90 percent of the law enforcement, court, and corrections activity in the United States is generated by drug users. This increased law enforcement activity has clogged our courts with drug-related cases and our prisons with drug offenders.

Substance abuse is a *political* issue which has increased the social and economic pressures already at work in our society. It has led elected officials to respond to public pressure to "do something" about drugs. Elected officials have responded by emphasizing drug abuse as a law enforcement and human service program issue and by diverting resources to address this issue. But at the same time, drug abuse has made it more difficult to successfully address other related law enforcement and public health issues. It has increased the cost of health care and resultant political pressures for cost containment. It has exacerbated pressures on juvenile justice and educational systems. It has increased the need for functional families at a time when drugs have diminished the capacity of families to function effectively as social units. Most significantly, it has led to widespread demands for action but little agreement upon effective strategies.

WHAT IS SOCIETY DOING ABOUT DRUG ABUSE?

It is important to note from the outset that while everyone recognizes the problems caused by substance abuse, there is little agreement on either the cause of these problems or the appropriate solutions. Four general types of solutions have been proposed, each based on different assumptions about the root causes of the substance abuse problem: controlling supply, epidemiological, controlling demand, and decriminalization. Each of these will be discussed in turn below.

Thus far, the major effort against drugs has been a highly publicized but ineffective effort by the federal government to reduce the drug supply through interdiction of drug shipments and by state and local governments' increased police activity. These efforts have not succeeded, nor do they show any signs of doing so in the future. At the federal level, impartial observers conclude that the more than $21 billion that the federal government has spent for anti-drug efforts over the past eight years has been spent slowly, in varied directions, through tortuous layers of government, with scant evaluation of what works and what does not.[10] This includes $7.1 billion for border interdiction, $3.8 for domestic investigation, $2.4 billion for drug abuse prevention, $2.4 billion for drug abuse treatment, $2.2 billion for prisons, $1.1 billion for international investigations, and $1 billion for prosecution. Because the high level of public concern with drug abuse makes the war on drugs a politically irresistible effort, lawmakers have used it to push pet projects in their jurisdictions, turn hearings into morality plays aimed at TV audiences, and fragment responsibility for substance abuse among dozens of unrelated agencies.[11] There are even increasing indications that the war on drugs will become real, with increased involvement by the American military forces in defoliation, interdiction, and intelligence operations. This alteration of long-standing prohibitions against the military's engaging in civilian law enforcement functions, supported by both advocates of civil liberties and military policymakers, is in itself an indication of how desperate the war on drugs has become.[12]

But in fact, it is fair to conclude that these efforts have been both ineffective and misdirected. They may be considered ineffective because the supply of illegal drugs has not decreased over the past ten years. Rather, the quality of cocaine and marijuana has improved, the manufacture of "crack" cocaine has blossomed into a major underground industry, and the street price of illegal drugs continues to fall. This is due to what economists would consider predictable results of attempts to restrict the supply of drugs. As popular demand continues, government pressure upon producers and suppliers has led to increased competition, and thus to the development of better armed and organized drug dealers. The Bush administration has attempted to refocus the effort by punishing users and middlemen, though it is uncertain where funds will come from for the police, court, and prison expenses associated with this effort.[13] Other related efforts include denying driver licenses or school loans to drug users. And it is misdirected in that the drug of choice, alcohol, is not even a target. While advertisers support battling drug abuse (because they lose no accounts in this war), they are uneasy about restricting advertising for alcoholic beverage companies, which spend hundreds of millions of dollars annually on advertising. And these companies (whether because they are public service oriented or because they want to reduce demand for illegal drugs as a competitor to alcohol) are also heavy contributors to anti-drug campaigns. One, Philip Morris, has placed and paid for $310 million worth of anti-drug ads in the past two years.[14]

A second front in the war on drugs has been the public health approach, which considers substance abuse to be a community health or epidemiologic issue like hepatitis, measles, or influenza. This model has much to recommend it, including a heavy contribution from the existing theory of alcohol abuse. This model considers substance abuse to be a disease, caused by a combination of genetic and environmental factors. In the short run, it proposes that substance abuse be attacked by community screening, education, and treatment programs. In the long run, it even offers the possibility that genetic replacement may eliminate the problem, much as "gene splicing" may in the future eliminate such genetically caused disabilities as multiple sclerosis.[15] But the model has detractors. Most people are uncomfortable with the way it glosses over the issue of individual responsibility and choice. Substance abuse, after all, requires many conscious choices over a long period of time, while communicable diseases are primarily transmitted unconsciously and involuntarily. Then, too, substance abuse has a more pervasive impact on social, economic, and political systems than do other public health issues (with the possible exception of AIDS). And the resources needed to treat substance abuse as a national epidemic are simply not forthcoming. New York City, for example, provides free drug treatment to fewer than one in ten of its addicts.[16] In this context, the idea of genetic change appears both too far in the future for serious consideration and too politically extreme because of its totalitarian and eugenic implications.

The third approach to reducing societal substance abuse requires a hard look at why individuals choose to abuse substances or to stop doing so. Most bluntly, this approach holds that the key to the substance abuse problem is to reverse the trends that have destroyed inner-city neighborhoods over the past twenty years. Drugs have made these neighborhoods worse, but poor housing, education, and community services have played a more fundamental role. This resulted from our fixation with winning the cold war against communism, and our resultant misplacement of budget priorities.[17]

Along with this emphasis on demand, some reasonable observers favor legalization or decriminalization of drugs. They point to the United States' experience with Prohibition, showing that efforts to restrict supply only succeeded in building criminal empires, increasing bootlegging profits, and driving drinkers from beer and wine onto the "hard stuff." They conclude that our war on drugs is having the same effect. Legalization would enable governments to tax sales and use the revenues for drug education and treatment programs. It would also reduce the amount spent on interdiction, investigation, prosecution, and corrections, and it would reduce the societal violence resulting from underworld competition for a vast and immensely profitable business.[18] These observers feel that all drugs are dangerous, but that legalization (in combination with education and treatment for abusers) is the most rational approach to the problem.[19] Also, decriminalization of intoxicants would shift the focus of concern to the individual's responsibility for the costs caused by substance abuse, rather than simply involve the user in the criminal justice system. For example, one state requires drunk drivers to pay for the cost of injuries suffered in an auto accident if the driver has a prior conviction for the offense.[20]

But it is doubtful that any public policy which accepts the continued use of drugs among the general population will gain widespread acceptance. Abuse of any substance reduces the individual's effectiveness in social relationships, school, or employment, and some drugs which are now illegal or controlled (such as "crack," "angel dust," or amphetamines) may cause violent and irrational behavior. For whatever reason, our society's experience with the consequences of individual experimentation with drugs has not resulted in greater public acceptance of recreational drugs. Legalization is opposed by people who understand that drug use is bad and fear that legalization will make it worse.

Yet the abysmal failure of efforts to interdict and otherwise control the supply of drugs over a long period of time has led many reputable observers to consider legalization the only alternative that makes sense.[21] George Shultz, former secretary of state, recently remarked that:

> I welcome the emphasis that is now being put on the drug problem. The efforts—to get to the people who are addicted, try to rehabilitate them; if they cannot be rehabilitated, at least to contain them; to educate people, to strongly discourage use of drugs by people who are casual users and first users, to stop this process among the young—all of these things I think are extremely important.
>
> But I have to tell you that it seems to me that the conceptual base of the current program is flawed and the program is not likely to work. . . .
>
> These efforts wind up creating a market where the price vastly exceeds the cost. With these incentives, demand creates its own supply and a criminal network along with it. . . .

We need at least to consider and examine forms of controlled legalization of drugs.

I find it very difficult to say that. Sometimes at a reception or cocktail party I advance these views and people head for somebody else. . . . No politician wants to say what I just said, not for a minute.[22]

After looking at these options, many reasonable observers conclude that we can't think of substance abuse as a single problem. Some users, particularly of legal drugs such as alcohol, tend to live within the mainstream and operate in more or less rational ways. As it becomes evident that drugs are destructive and wrong, these people are using drugs less or avoiding drugs altogether. For this group, education and treatment become the public policy choice. And many policies now being considered by state governments are intended to make it more likely that rational "casual users" will avoid drugs. For example, Florida's governor has proposed that first-time applicants for driver licenses in the state be required to pass a drug test.[23] And Arizona tries to deter "recreational" drug use by treating those arrested for possession of small amounts of illegal drugs to the jail terms and fines usually reserved for drug traffickers and career criminals.[24] And the number of recreational drug users whose behavior may be changed by such policies may not be great. Research on the cocaine market shows that people who use it once a week or less make up only 10 percent to 15 percent of the total demand for the drug.[25] And one of the local judges most heavily involved in the program concludes, "I do get the occasional yuppie now and then as a result of the anti-user crackdown. But the huge majority are still young, black. They don't have jobs, they don't have skills, they don't want treatment, they don't care about a criminal record."[26] For persons such as these who don't act in their self interest and persist in self-destructive behavior, some combination of punishment and epidemiological treatment may be the best answer. Drug czar William Bennett calls it a "crisis of authority," and he is right. But it is also a crisis in hope—in the distribution of income and in perceptions people have about their chances of getting ahead in American society.[27]

Substance abuse has been recognized as a serious societal problem for many years. Yet there is no agreement on its causes or on an appropriate solution.

SUBSTANCE ABUSE IN THE WORKPLACE

It is within this context of societal concern and uncertainty that workplace substance abuse must be addressed. Regardless of its causes, substance abuse raises three major concerns for American employers in both the public and the private sectors. Beyond its impact on the individual employee's personal accomplishments and social relationships, it has serious negative consequences for other employees and the organization. These problems are lost productivity, increased liability risks, and increased health care costs.

Productivity losses include those resulting from impaired performance, absenteeism, injuries, and fatalities.[28] One Fortune 500 company released profiles of the typical drug abuser indicating that, in comparison with the typical employee, this person functions at about 67 percent of potential, is 3.6 times as likely to be involved in an accident, receives three times the average level of health care benefits, is five times as likely to file a worker's compensation claim, more likely to file grievances, and misses more that ten times as many workdays![29]

It is estimated that between 12 percent and 15 percent of any given work force will be substance abusers at any one time.[30] And this does not include the 35 percent of the work force whose use of tobacco also raises health and productivity concerns. Experts estimate that employees who are substance abusers produce 30 to 35 percent less than other employees.[31] Beyond direct productivity impacts, studies have shown that employees do not like to work with other employees who are substance abusers. It tends to reduce their own morale and productivity. These costs add up—most knowledgeable observers say the annual toll in lost productivity is at least $100 billion. NIDA estimates $42 billion annually in lost production and higher medical bills.[32] The U.S. Chamber of Commerce claims $60–100 billion annually in lost productivity alone.[33] In data which are dated but still indicative of the extent of the problem, the Research Triangle Institute reported in 1986 that the cost of reduced productivity from alcohol abuse alone in 1980 was $50.6 billion, and an additional $25.7 billion for other drugs.[34] The National Institute on Alcohol Abuse and Alcoholism concludes that alcoholism accounts for about 105,000 deaths each year and will cost the nation an estimated $136 billion in lost employment, reduced productivity, and health care costs in 1990.[35] In 1983, from alcohol alone, there were 10 million injuries (2 million of which were disabling), and 18,000 fatalities.[36] And bad as the effects of substance abuse are for large corporations and government agencies, they can be worse for small family businesses because of close personal relationships and the perceived stigma of admitting a problem within the family ranks. One commentator concludes that "alcohol and other drugs can be a family's biggest competitor for profits and business longevity."[37]

While it is difficult to separate the effects of substance abuse from other causes of increased health care costs (such as changes in technology, the aging population, and the practice of defensive medicine) many observers claim that substance abuse also results in higher health care costs for employers. According to one estimate, it increased the cost of health insurance as much as 170 percent in three years for several major plans.[38] For a small firm, these increases in health benefit costs make the difference between profit and loss; they inevitably lead many companies to select plans with lower benefits,[39] to ask employees to assume more of the costs of health benefits,[40] to penalize those employees whose poor health care practices increase the cost of health benefits coverage,[41] or to drop employee health care coverage entirely. And this increase in health care costs has spawned a whole new industry, the utilization-review firms that audit medical costs to prevent unnecessary treatments or overpayments.[42]

Lastly, substance abuse increases liability risks for employers because of the increased chance of performance impairments, which will affect customers, co-workers, or the public.[43] These can include injuries or death resulting from assaults or accidents with vehicles and equipment. Our society is increasingly litigious, in that victims are much less willing to accept these things as an unavoidable part of life and much more likely to seek financial damages through the court system. Juries are much more likely to agree. And tort law (plus the universal practice of paying attorneys a percentage of the award on a contingency basis rather than on a fee-for-service basis) stipulates that if both the employee and the employer were responsible for the damage, judgments are levied proportionate with ability to pay rather than extent of liability. This doctrine of "deep pockets," as it is called, means that an employer who is ruled to be 1 percent liable for the acts of an employee may be required to pay 100 percent of the damages awarded to the victim of an employee's careless or criminal behavior. Under these circumstances, wealthy corporations or government agencies (who are able to pay large awards out of corporate equity or through the general taxing power of the state), have been required to pay tremendous awards in cases where most reasonable observers would have concluded they had only limited liability.

For example, a major private corporation recently paid millions of dollars to the victims and survivors of an auto accident caused by one of its employees. The circumstances? The employee had shown up for work intoxicated and had been immediately ordered to go home by the supervisor. The court ruled that even though the employee was primarily responsible for the accident, the employer was also responsible because the employee had been involved in the accident while following a supervisory order. A better supervisory response might have been to call a cab and put the employee in it!

FIGHTING SUBSTANCE ABUSE IN THE WORKPLACE

For these reasons, it is clear that employers have to do something about employee substance abuse. And from a national policy perspective, focusing on the workplace as one arena in which to address this issue is both necessary and reasonable. In terms of policy theory, the best strategy to adopt when you are faced with a problem you can't clearly define and solutions you don't know will work is to experiment with a variety of alternative approaches and pick the most promising ones.

Controlling workplace substance abuse is certainly defensible as one of the most rational societal policies for responding to substance abuse. Why? Our two best measures of persons' ability to function in society are whether they can maintain stable social relationships (family and friends) and hold a job. Inability to do these things means that there is an increased likelihood they will end up in jail or a psychiatric facility. Employees who have substance abuse problems already have much to lose by continued poor job performance. If they are at all rational, they will realize that loss of a job will make it much harder to continue substance abuse without running afoul of the criminal justice system. In addition, job loss will mean loss of status and self-respect. It will mark the passage from recreational drug use to dependence, from control of the drug habit to control by the drug habit.

From a public policy perspective, our demonstrated inability to limit the supply of drugs or to convince the disadvantaged that substance abuse is not a desirable alternative means that we have implicitly adopted different substance abuse policies for different social groups. First, for those who have good jobs or want them, we have tied employment in major corporations and public agencies with the ability to pass drug tests. Second, for those who do not have the skills or education enabling them to qualify for jobs with these first-tier employers, we are rapidly creating a larger pool of less attractive laborer and service positions. Employees in these positions usually do not have to pass drug screening programs as a condition of employment. But the positions have lower pay and benefits, less chance of continuity, and less chance of advancement to responsible technical and professional positions. The jobs are designed to limit the effects of employee substance abuse to the employer. For example, the jobs tend to be menial or routinized to reduce risk of poor performance caused by impairment. Health benefits are minimal or nonexistent, particularly if the employees are hired on a temporary, part-time, or hourly basis. And liability risks are reduced if they are hired through an employment service or a contractor who then assumes legal responsibility for their performance. And third, for those who cannot hold even these jobs, we offer a patchwork system of criminal justice and public welfare to protect these people from the consequences of their substance abuse if possible (through education and treatment) and to protect the rest of us from these consequences if not.

Briefly, major employers throughout the United States have responded to the problem of substance abuse by agreeing that a substance-abuse-free workplace is desirable. Then they have moved to create this by testing all applicants and, under some conditions, employees. Because random testing of all employees raises profound issues of employees' legal rights, testing in public agencies was initiated by the federal government for military personnel (whose constitutional protections against due process and invasion of privacy are quite circumscribed already by the Uniform Code of Military Justice). Testing first occurred in 1981, followed by testing of civilian employees within the Department of Defense in 1985 under Directive 1010.[44] In September 1986, President Reagan expanded substance abuse testing of federal employees by issuing Executive Order 12564 ("Federal Agency Drug-Free Workplace Act"). This order provided for mandatory drug testing for federal employees occupying sensitive positions—those with access to classified data or those considered to affect public health and safety. State and local governments followed, particularly for police officers and public transit drivers.

In the private sector, employers are much more able to implement testing procedures, since these employers do not have to fulfill the stricter constitutional standards to which the public employer is held.[45] The number of companies testing applicants or employees for substance abuse increased from 5 percent in 1982 to 40 percent in 1987. According to the Department of Labor, 20 percent of all American workers are now employed by companies that test for drug use.[46] Testing of applicants rose to 25 percent in 1988.[47]

Substance abuse testing is an invasive and dehumanizing procedure which generally degrades the relationship between employer and employees. Given that this is true, it is remarkable and depressing that major employers have adopted substance abuse testing so quickly and uniformly, especially considering its profound impact on employee rights, personnel practices, collective bargaining agreements, and other aspects of personnel management. A recent poll commissioned by the Institute for a Drug-Free Workplace (affiliated with the U.S. Chamber of Commerce) reported that 41 percent of the approximately 1,000 employees surveyed said drug use by employees seriously affects their ability to get the job done. Ninety-seven percent said drug testing of employees is appropriate under at least some circumstances, regardless of reservations they may have about testing.[48] And drug testing has been widely adopted not only in the private sector, where employees have fewer constitutional protections of privacy and due process, but also in public agencies, where civil service systems and collective bargaining agreements have made it much more difficult to discipline or discharge unproductive employees.

SUMMARY

Substance abuse is the major domestic problem and perhaps the most important public policy issue facing Americans today. Politically, the war on drugs is a highly publicized campaign and a convincingly documented failure. Economically, it costs the country over $100 billion annually in lost productivity and increased health care costs. Socially, it makes our already inadequate human service programs less effective—education, employment, housing, community services, and health services among them. It burdens our law enforcement, courts, and corrections systems with drug-related offenders. Politically, it has increased the gap between the "haves" and the "have nots," and led to proposed solutions which threaten historic constitutional rights to privacy.

The four policies we have considered societally for dealing with substance abuse are controlling supply, epidemiological, controlling demand, and decriminalization. These policies have either failed to work, failed to win political support, or failed to win the resources needed for a realistic test of their effectiveness.

Workplace substance abuse is a major issue for employers because it results in lower employee productivity, increased health care costs, and increased liability risks. Given the uncertainties of national substance abuse policies, most major private and public employers have developed rational substance abuse policies for their individual workplaces. These policies implement drug testing for applicants and employees. They guarantee applicants that substance abusers will not be hired. They offer help to employees who have substance abuse problems, but also threaten to fire them if the problem continues.

Because jobs are so important to employees, it makes sense for employers to use substance abuse testing and the threat of job loss as a means of reducing workplace substance abuse. But keep in mind that while this element of our national substance abuse policy is necessary, it is not sufficient—it will not work with the majority of Americans who are not yet in the first-tier labor market or are already out of it.

NOTES

1. National Institute on Drug Abuse. (1988). *National Household Survey on Drug Abuse: Main Findings, 1985*. U.S. Department of Health and Human Services, Public Health Service, Alcohol, Drug Abuse and Mental Health Administration.

2. U.S. Department of Health and Human Services, National Institute on Drug Abuse. (1987). *Research on the Prevalence, Impact and Treatment of Drug Abuse in the Workplace*, Announcement No. DA-87-26.

3. Kaufman, A. (1986, October 19). The battle over drug testing. *New York Times*, Section 6 (Magazine), p. 54.

4. Wrich, J. (1988, January–February). Beyond testing: Coping with drugs at work. *Harvard Business Review*, 120–127, 130–131.

5. National Institute on Drug Abuse. (1988). *National Household Survey*.

6. National Institute on Drug Abuse. (1988). *National Household Survey*, p. 98.

7. McQueen, M., & Shribman, D. (1989, September 20). Battle against drugs is chief issue facing nation, Americans say. *The New York Times*, p. 1.

8. News briefs. (1989, February). *Business and Health*, p. 6.

9. Singh, H. (1990, May 1). To lower infant mortality rate, get mothers off drugs. *The Wall Street Journal*, p. A-18.

10. Barrett, P. (1989, September 1). Federal war on drugs is a scattershot affair, with dubious progress. *The Wall Street Journal*, p. 1.

11. Yang, J. E., & Barrett, P. (1989, September 6). Drug issue triggers Washington habit: Turf wars in Congress, administration. *The Wall Street Journal*, p. A-20.

12. Sharpe, K., & Blachman, M. (1990, March 25). Sacrificing liberties to the drug war. *The Miami Herald*, p. 14.

13. Barrett, P. (1990, January 26). Bush proposes to boost appropriations for anti-drug campaign by $1.2 billion. *The Wall Street Journal*, p. A-18.

14. Lipman, J. (1990, February 23). Lumping alcohol into drug war isn't idea industry's warming to. *The Wall Street Journal*, p. B-5.

15. Nazario, S. (1990, April 18). Alcohol is linked to a gene. *The Wall Street Journal*, p. B-1.

16. Lewis, A. (1989, August 16). Drugs: Don't listen to Dr. Feelgood. *The Wall Street Journal*, p. 25A.

17. Drugs: Why not? (1989, August 31). *The Wall Street Journal*, p. A14.

18. Cockburn, A. (1989, September 7). From Andes to inner cities, cocaine is a good career choice. *The Wall Street Journal*, p. A15; The devil you know. (1989, December 29). *The Wall Street Journal*, p. A6; and It doesn't have to be like this. (1989, September 2). *The Economist*, p. 21.

19. Wisotsky, S. (1986). *Breaking the impasse in the war on drugs*. New York: Greenwood Press.

20. Making drunk drivers pay for their injuries. (1990, February 28). *The Wall Street Journal*, p. B1.

21. Shultz on drug legalization. (1989, October 27). *The Wall Street Journal*, p. A16.

22. Ibid.

23. Drug test urged for drivers. (1989, February 10). *The Miami Herald*, p. 1A.

24. Barrett, P. (1990, January 31). Yuppie nightmare: Program to prosecute the casual drug user is casting wider net. *The Wall Street Journal*, p. A20.

25. Ibid.

26. Ibid.

27. Drug ups, and downs. (1989, July 19). *The Wall Street Journal*, p. A14.

28. Lodge, J. (1987). Drugs: Abuse is an economic issue. *Credit*, 13, pp. 28–29.

29. Greenberg, E. (1987). To test or not to test: drugs and the workplace. *Management Review*, p. 24.

30. Delaney, Jr., T. J. (1987). The EAP part of the personnel function. *Public Personnel Management*, p. 359.

31. Nutile, T. (1988, February 1). Business battles enemy that costs $71 billion. *Boston Herald*, p. 2.

32. Lyons, P. V. (March 1987). EAPs the only real cure. *Management Review*, p. 38.

33. Rosen, T. H. (Fall 1987). Identification of substance abusers in the workplace. *Public Personnel Management* 16 (3), p. 200.

34. Ibid., p. 198.

35. Nazario, S. (1990, April 18). Alcohol is linked to a gene. *The Wall Street Journal*, p. B1.

36. Rosen. Identification of substance abusers. p. 198.

37. Bork, D. (1986, December). Drug abuse in the family business. *Nation's Business*, p. 60.

38. Donkin, R. (1989, April). New hope for diagnosing alcoholism. *Business & Health*, pp. 20-23.

39. Ricklefs, R. (1988, December 6). Health insurance becomes a big pain for small firms. *The Wall Street Journal*, p. B1.

40. Karr, A. & Carnevale, M. L. (1989, August 11). Facing off over health-care benefits: Companies ask workers to pay more of costs. *The Wall Street Journal*, p. B1.

41. Rundle, R. (1990, February 14). U-Haul puts high price on vices of its workers. *The Wall Street Journal*, pp. B1, 10.

42. Robichaux, M. (1989, September 6). Soaring health-care costs spur entrepreneurial fever. *The Wall Street Journal*, p. B2.

43. Klingner, D. (1988). The personal liability of state and local personnel directors: Legal, organizational, and ethical implications. *Public Personnel Management*, 17(1), pp. 125–133.

44. Department of Defense Directive 1010.9 as cited in National Federation of Government Employees v. Weinberger, 640 F. Supp. 642 (D.C. Cir. 1986), rev'd and remanded, 919 f.2nd 935 (D.C. Cir. 1987).

45. United States v. Cruikshank, 92 U.S. 542 (1875).

46. Dillon, J. (1987, May 24). How IBM uses its influence to shape drug-testing bill. *Rutland* (Vermont) *Daily Herald*, p. 1.

47. Chaves, T. (1989, January 27). Doubling in drug testing reported. (Oklahoma City) *Daily Oklahoman*, p. 1.

48. Drug use on job worries many workers, poll says. (1989, December 14). *The Wall Street Journal*, p. B1.

2

Substance Abuse
Testing Techniques

Substance abuse tests are used to determine which applicants or employees use alcohol or other drugs. These tests, particularly the urine tests used to detect abuse of prescription and illegal drugs, are understandably the most visible and highly publicized aspect of an employer's substance abuse policy. After all, most employees feel that being required to provide a urine sample as a condition of employment is a distasteful violation of their right to personal and medical privacy. And if the results of the urinalysis are used as the basis for discharge or disciplinary action against employees who are satisfactory performers, those employees are likely to feel that the tests violate their rights to due process or are self-incriminating.

While this chapter focuses initially on the so-called "nuts and bolts" or actual methodologies for testing employee usage of drugs, it also addresses the validity issues inherent whenever drug testing comes under serious consideration for an organization. For there probably is no other area that potentially carries such enormous consequences for the individual being tested. We can use a simple 2 x 2 table to illustrate the point. Analyzing this table, we note that the substance abuser who tests positive may indeed be the most fortunate. Through confrontation and the of-

Table 2
Test Findings and Organizational Outcome Implications

	Organizational Outcome Implications:	
	For Substance Abusers	For Substance Non-Abusers
Test Findings:		
Positive:	confrontation, possible job loss, chance for rehabilitation	confrontation, possible job loss if employer does not adequately confirm positive test results
Negative:	continued low job performance, possible job loss with no job-based treatment option	none

fering of treatment services, he may be able to return to a more normal, functional lifestyle while salvaging his job. A false negative may delay confrontation, but without a known reason for poor job performance, he may eventually lose his job and the benefit of treatment supported (financially and otherwise) by his employer. But clearly, the individual who is not a substance abuser and unfortunately receives a false positive on testing also is at risk.

It is in this area of validity and reliability that organizations carry the greatest responsibility for providing testing methodologies which are the most reliable and valid available within modern technology. The organization must have very specific and well-defined procedures for verifying positive test results with the highest possible degree of accuracy. While employer responsibility is primarily at an ethical level, potential litigation is a strong factor for consideration as well.

Therefore, if an employer makes the decision to combat workplace substance abuse by instituting a testing program, it is important that testing procedures be accurate (valid and reliable). It is also critical that the laboratory which conducts the tests have a proven track record which ensures protection and documentation of the "chain of custody" for samples.

OBJECTIVES

The purpose of this chapter is to:

1. Define substance abuse.
2. Describe and evaluate the noninvasive tests used to detect substance abuse.

3. Describe and evaluate the laboratory tests used to detect substance abuse through analysis of urine.

4. Describe and evaluate the other laboratory tests used to detect substance abuse, including the breathalyzer for alcohol and hair samples for other drugs.

5. Discuss testing procedures and evaluate these tests with respect to their comparative validity, reliability, and cost.

6. Tell how to select a testing laboratory so that the testing methodology ensures that the collection, handling, analysis, and storage of samples are performed so as to protect their integrity.

WHAT IS SUBSTANCE ABUSE?

The medical community has led the way in helping human resource managers and supervisors understand characteristics of drug pattern usage. Psychiatrists, in particular those working in the field of substance abuse, make clear distinctions between drug use, drug abuse, and drug dependence.[1] Very specific diagnostic criteria have been established which allow the clinician to minimize subjectivity and make the appropriate diagnosis based upon clearly defined standards. In is important to realize that these diagnostic criteria recognize socio-cultural as well as physiologic dimensions.

Substance abuse has been defined by the American Psychiatric Association as "a maladaptive pattern of substance use lasting at least a month" and indicated by at least one of the following:[2]

1. Continued use despite knowledge of having a persistent or recurrent social, occupational, psychological, or physical problem that is caused or exacerbated by use of the psychoactive substance;

2. Recurrent use in situations in which use is physically hazardous (e.g., driving while intoxicated or a diabetic using alcoholic drinks when they are clearly contraindicated in diabetes).

Criteria are also clearly defined for drug dependence and relate to an individual's inability to have control over the substance and an obsessive preoccupation with it. The criteria include at least three of the following:

1. Substance often taken in larger amounts or over a longer period than the person intended.

2. Persistent desire or one or more unsuccessful efforts to cut down or control substance use.

3. A great deal of time spent in activities necessary to get the substance (e.g., theft), taking the substance (e.g., chain smoking), or recovering from its effects.

4. Frequent intoxication or withdrawal symptoms when expected to fulfill major role obligations at work, school, or home (e.g., doesn't go to work because hung over, goes to school or work "high," intoxicated while taking care of children), or substance use in physically hazardous situations.

5. Important social, occupational, or recreational activities given up or reduced because of substance use.

6. Continued substance use despite knowledge of having a persistent or recurrent social, psychological, or physical problem that is caused or exacerbated by the use of the substance (e.g., keeps using heroin despite family arguments about it, cocaine-induced depression, or having an ulcer made worse by drinking).

7. Marked tolerance—need for markedly increased amounts of the substance (i.e., at least a 50 percent increase) in order to achieve intoxication or desired effect, or markedly diminished effect with continued use of the same amount.

8. Characteristic withdrawal symptoms.

9. Substance often taken to relieve or avoid withdrawal symptoms.

The last three criteria are relatively specific to physiologically addictive substances and therefore do not necessarily apply to marijuana, hallucinogens, PCP, and cocaine.

Probably the most significant point to this discussion is the fact that the criteria listed above are based upon observable behavior rather than upon a toxicologic examination or subjective impressions. *The problem of workplace substance abuse is best identified and addressed by observable behavior in the workplace—by work performance!* Drug tests are unable to distinguish among drug use, abuse, and dependence. Nor are the tests able to determine the performance abilities of the employee.

However, in considering job performance, it is more than clear that the active use of drugs does impact directly on how the job gets done. Drug levels which bring about intoxication will impair function. Cocaine, for example, which acts over a relatively short period, usually causes substantial mood swings which range from elation to depression, irritability, and even more seriously, overt paranoia. Alcohol abuse also is highly associated with violent and unpredictable behavior. Employees who are undergoing withdrawal quite obviously would be unable to concentrate on the work at hand, rather concentrating on how to obtain the next supply of drugs. This behavior often includes buying and even possibly selling of drugs in the workplace, behavior highly disruptive to workplace productivity.

For the employer who appropriately focuses upon observable work performance, there must an accompanying educational component for employees and their frontline supervisors. The educational component should be strong and extensive and include information on substance abuse as well as the identification of substandard work performance possibly due to substance abuse. Performance evaluations which are standardized and consistent are, of course, essential. Drug testing, then, without educational, behavioral observation, and solid evaluation components, assumes a disciplinary, punitive posture which is adversarial in nature.

NONINVASIVE TESTING PROCEDURES

The initial discussion on determing whether or not employees are abusing drugs will begin not with describing current methods of analysis of body fluids such as urine or blood serum, or even of the newer methods of saliva or hair analysis, but on less invasive options: direct questioning and questionnaires. It will then progress to a discussion of laboratory testing procedures.

Direct Questioning

The direct questioning of the employee regarding frequency and quantity of alcohol and/or drug consumption can be an important method for detecting substance abuse and dependency. This is long-established, common practice within the medical community. While some studies have shown that patients do accurately describe their amount of alcohol use, there are definite problems with reliability.[3] Underestimation may occur for a variety of reasons which may be as simple as forgetfulness or may be directly attributable to the psychological defense known as denial. Employees could be expected to show a much greater reticence to acknowledge substantial drug use/abuse for fear of retaliatory or punitive measures by the employer. One study which addressed the question of frequency and amount of alcohol consumption found a sensitivity of less than 50 percent in detecting persons with a drinking problem, when it was evaluated against the Michigan Alcoholism Screening Test (MAST).[4] Researchers also estimate the sensitivity of historical inquiry to be as low as 10 percent to 15 percent.[5] Review of additional articles within journals of alcohol studies and addictions appear to find most experts in agreement that asking patients about their use of alcohol and drugs is at best highly variable and depends in large part on the patient, the skills of the interviewer, and other individual circumstances.

The medical community has had extensive experience in direct questioning, with mixed results. But this method may still be a useful tool within the workplace. If questioning is done in a direct and honest manner, with assurances given that the employer is committed to the goals of education, prevention, and rehabilitation (where applicable), questioning may indeed be the most simple, least invasive, least costly, and most effective substance abuse testing method.

Questionnaires

Questionnaires have been developed which have been extensively evaluated for detecting alcohol abuse. Again, their use has been predominantly within the gen-

Table 3
CAGE Test for Alcohol Abuse

C:	Have you ever felt you ought to Cut down on drinking?
A:	Have people Annoyed you by criticizing your drinking?
G:	Have you ever felt bad or Guilty about your drinking?
E:	Have you ever had a drink first thing in the morning to steady your nerves or get rid of a hangover (Eye-opener)?

eral field of medicine and most specifically within the addiction field.[6] The most common of these tests include the MAST, the CAGE questionnaire, and the Self-Administered Alcoholism Screening Test (SAAST). The original MAST is very lengthy, but an abbreviated version known as the Brief MAST (BMAST) has been developed. The sensitivity of the test is reported to be 84 percent to 100 percent, while the specificity is said to be from 87 percent to 95 percent.[7]

However, the most commonly used questionnaire in primary medical practice is the CAGE instrument, which is only four questions. Its brevity and simplicity no doubt accounts for its popularity. Sensitivities have been reported as high as 85 percent to 89 percent and as low as 49 percent to 68 percent. Specificity has been reported as high as 79 percent to 95 percent.[8] An example of the CAGE is given in Table 3.

The inconsistencies in reports on the CAGE as well as the other questionnaires are due to numerous reasons. Populations under study can vary enormously. Consistent difficulties arise in standardizing definitions of problem drinking, especially before significant changes in behavior begin.

While alcohol screening tests have been extensively evaluated, there are few reliable questionnaires available which detect drug abuse other than alcohol. A questionnaire known as the Addiction Severity Index is used in the drug abuse field to evaluate the treatment needs of patients with signs of drug/alcohol abuse or dependence.[9]

LABORATORY TESTS

The medical community has developed laboratory analytic methods for screening body fluids as another method to detect drug and alcohol abuse. The actual technology has developed for well over twenty years. The locus of development was the medical field. Its primary purpose was to aid in diagnosis and treatment for drug overdoses and to aid in treatment in drug rehabilitation programs.

When laboratory testing is discussed for workplace settings, we generally mean urine toxicology, though more sophisticated methods continue to be developed such as testing of human hair and saliva. This type of testing is in relatively early developmental stages and there are some researchers and clinicians who feel testing of hair, for instance, is an even more invasive procedure than urine or even blood tests.

Blood tests are probably used for detecting alcohol more frequently than for the detection of drugs. But for testing of alcohol in the workplace, the breathalyzer is probably the most preferred because it is the least invasive. With the breathalyzer observation is simplified, as is the chain of custody. However, there are decidedly different findings in state court rulings around the country, and positive tests may not be evidentiary in certain cases unless there is a supporting positive blood test and/or the person admits to alcohol consumption.

In medical practice, physicians also use other tests that detect bodily dysfunctions associated with chronic alcohol abuse. For example, with chronic alcohol abuse, an increase in hepatic (liver) enzymes is frequently found, as well as an elevation in the erythrocyte mean corpuscular volume (a specific test on the red blood cells). However, because these are not consistent findings, they cannot be used as strong screening tests for alcoholism.

The test considered to be the most sensitive for alcohol abuse is known as the serum gamma-glutamyl transferase (GGT), and some studies find the sensitivity as high as 60 percent. However, the specificity is generally poor due to GGT elevation which can occur because of certain medications and various medical conditions such as diabetes and heart or kidney disease. As a result, false positives have been reported to be as high as 13 percent to 50 percent.[10]

Current research revolves around statistical analysis which attempts to combine these various biochemical tests with information garnered from interviews and questionnaires. It is hoped the analysis will enhance the ability to predict alcoholism with much greater accuracy.

Biological testing also provides evidence of drug use other than alcohol. For example, in chronic abuse of cocaine and heroin, particularly with intravenous use, there are certain enzymes which can become markedly elevated. However, sensitivity can again be very poor due to the elevation of these specific enzymes as a result of other serious medical conditions. With due consideration given that these tests are not included in the routine drug testing used in the workplace, i.e., urine testing, they can conceivably be performed during the annual physical examination and be used by employers as additional evidence of chronic substance abuse.

TYPES OF URINE TESTS USED TO DETECT SUBSTANCE ABUSE IN THE WORKPLACE

When discussion proceeds on substance abuse testing in the workplace, it almost always relates to tests conducted on urine. Interestingly, the tests are designed to detect a wide range of drugs, including alcohol, of course, but not focusing on it. Alcohol testing differs in several ways from that of other abusive drugs. Alcohol is the most widely abused of all drugs in our society, if one does not include tobacco use. Because alcohol is a legal substance, its presence in a urine sample does not necessarily indicate illegal behavior. In addition, alcohol has a well-established level that is legally considered to be intoxication; this is not so for the majority of the other drugs under discussion. And finally, issues on the reliability and accuracy of tests for alcohol have been relatively settled within the legal and scientific communities, while they clearly have not been for the range of illegal drugs.

The following is a description of the most commonly performed chromatographic and immunoassay procedures that are used to detect the presence of abusive drugs.

Thin-Layer Chromatography (TLC)

Thin-Layer Chromatography (TLC) is one of the oldest techniques of drug analysis. It is also the least expensive. The technique involves the use of an absorbent material such as silica which is commonly affixed to a material such as glass. Drops of the sample as well as standards of known content and concentration are applied to the absorbent material. This is then immersed in a solvent solution which passes through the absorbent matter. Separation of the components of the sample and the standard occur due to their different solubilities. The result is that they then occupy different areas on the TLC plate. The plate is dried and then one or more reagents are applied, which produces a color. The presence of a drug is read as positive if a spot of the appropriate color appears in a location which corresponds to the drug(s) present in the standard.

A major problem with TLC is that interpretation of the results requires the presence of a technician with considerable skill and experience to run the test. In addition, characteristics of the drug and/or its metabolites can cause subtle shades of color difference or spot position which may also be interpreted differently by different technicians. A major advantage of the TLC is its low cost as well as its ability to screen for several drugs simultaneously. However, while TLC is still commonly used in some forensic situations, it has moved to a secondary position in most drug testing situations because of the need for the technician's expertise and its lack of sensitivity to certain drugs.

Newer techniques appear to combine some of the simplicity and low costs of the original tests but are higher in sensitivity. These are known as Bonded-Phase TLC (BPTLC) and High-Performance TLC (HPTLC).[11]

Radioimmunoassay (RIA)

Radioimmunoassays (RIAs) use specific antibodies which are a response to drugs and/or their metabolites. An assorted number of radioactive labels indicate a specific drug is present. The commonly used RIA kits have a shelf life of about two months, which is much shorter than the other immunoassay kits. However, the radioactivity allows for a significantly greater range of the assay, which in turn provides for greater sensitivity. Antibody formation causes radioactivity in a precipitate which may then be measured with an instrument known as a gamma counter. The amount of drug present is indicated by the amount of precipitated radioactivity.

A significant drawback with the RIA is that the test is labor intensive and therefore is not readily applicable in a high-volume automation situation. In addition, a

special laboratory is required because of the radioactive materials used. Technicians must be specially trained as well as have a license to work with radioactive
materials. However, RIA is one of the earliest immunoassay techniques, and it has
withstood an extensive period of evaluation.

Fluoroimmunoassay (FIA)

Fluoroimmunoassays (FIAs) utilize antibodies to measure barbiturates, cocaine,
and amphetamines by an unusual homogenous method which uses only a single
reagent. Due to different cutoff values used in this technique, the accuracy and reliability are reportedly difficult to determine. The commercial application of the
FIA is known as a "TDx" assay. The test does not find use in high-volume automated situations, and there is only one instrument that is currently used.

Enzyme Immunoassay (EIA)

Enzyme Immunoassays (EIAs) also have a long history for testing of abused
drugs. The enzyme-multiplied immunoassay technique, known as EMIT, is well-
known and the most widely used as an initial test. EMIT is considered to be a
highly sensitive test and specific for drugs or certain drug classes, depending on
the assay utilized. In this test, antibodies attach to the drug and form a complex.
The complex inhibits a secondary enzyme-substrate reaction which then brings
about an absorbance of light. The light in turn is measured by an instrument called
a spectrophotometer. The test also can be used with high volumes and with various
types of instruments. Evaluation of the EMIT has gone on for over a ten-year period.

Gas Chromatography (GC)

This test, also known as gas liquid chromatography (GLC), works by separating
substances from the sample. As the separation increases due to gases and heat, the
substances form in a chromatographic column. A recent enhancement to the technique has been the application of capillary columns. This detection that occurs at
the end of the columns is a great improvement from the previous assays. GC is used
not only as a confirmatory test, but is also used currently as an initial one for selected drugs.

A major problem with the GC is that it is slow because of the time required for
preparation as well as the time needed for extraction. Another problem that has
been identified is that in certain instances, the single value of column retention time
cannot be used to provide unequivocal identification.[12]

High-Performance Liquid Chromatography (HPLC)

High-Performance Liquid Chromatography uses many of the same principles of
chromatography methods described above. HPLC is generally able to measure

more than one compound at a time and is considered to be a good technique for confirming several drugs or drug metabolites. Among the detection methods used in this procedure are ultraviolet, fluorescence, and electrochemical detectors.

Gas Chromatography with Mass Spectrometry (GC/MS)

GC/MS is considered the state of the art in drug testing methods. It is also known as the "gold standard" for confirmatory testing. Mass spectrometry acts as the detection method at the end of the gas chromatography column. With this method there has been a dramatic increase in both the sensitivity and specificity of confirmatory testing capabilities. During the detection process itself ionization of the drug or its metabolites forms a "fingerprint" of the drug. Either electron impact or chemical ionization may be used, and the monitoring of ions and ion ratios results in a greatly decreased potential for interferences. While many believe that the reliability of GC/MS lies within the instrument itself, this is not so. It is much more dependent on the skill and experience of the technician as well as on the procedures of extraction and derivatization that are used on the sample. An almost constant updating with the complex procedures also seeks to improve the sensitivity as well as to simplify the analytic techniques themselves. The test is the most costly of all to perform.[13] Table 4 provides an overview of the detection limits of commonly abused drugs.[14]

DRUG TESTING METHODS OTHER THAN URINE TESTING

While urine testing is clearly the most common method used for testing workplace drug abuse, other methodologies are also used. Some of these are old and well-established, while others are only now being developed.

Breath Alcohol Analysis/Blood Alcohol Analysis

Concentration of alcohol in the breath or blood as measured through analysis serves as the basis for medicolegal alcohol determination purposes. In addition

> It is well established and universally accepted that the concentration of alcohol in the blood or breath, properly determined and interpreted, constitutes the best and most objective indicator of the absence or presence and degree of acute alchol-induced impairment of driving ability in living subjects.[15]

In the United States, the Intoximeter (breathalyzer) is the most widely used method to determine the BAC (blood alcohol concentration) for evidential purposes. This means that the results of the breath analysis act as estimates for the actual BAC. This presumes that there is a constant relationship between the BAC and the BrAC (breath alcohol concentration).

Table 4
Detection Limits of Commonly Abused Drugs

Drug:	Limits of sensitivity (micrograms/ml)	Approximate duration of detectability (days)
Amphetamine	0.5	2
Methamphetamine	0.5	2
Barbiturates:		
Short-Acting:		1
Hexobarbital	1.0	
Pentobarbital	0.5	
Secobarbital	0.5	
Thiamylal	1.0	
Immediate-Acting:		2–3
Amobarbital	1.0	
Aprobarbital	1.5	
Butabarbital	0.5	
Butabital	1.5	
Long-Acting:		<7
Barbital	5.0	
Phenobarbital	1.0	
Benzodiazepines	1.0	3
Cocaine metabolites:		2–3
Benzoylecgonine	1.0	
Ecgonine methyl ester	1.0	
Methadone	0.5	3
Codeine	0.5	2
Propoxphene	0.5	1–2
Cannabinoids	20mg/ml	3–5
Methaqualone	1.0	<7
Phencyclidine PCP	0.5	8 36

Marajuana

However, there are disagreements concerning the relationship between BAC and BrAC and the relationship of either indicator to driving impairment. Recent studies have found that the breath analysis tests may underestimate or overestimate the actual BAC.[16] In a research study done in 1985, after comprehensive review, the researcher concluded that epidemiological and laboratory results are consistent in supporting the use of 0.10 percent (weight/volume) as the BAC at which impairment of driving ability may be presumed.[17] However, a 1986 study recommended that the American Medical Association adopt a BAC of only 0.05 percent for the criminalization of driving. Additional research studies supported various other ranges.

As a result of the inconsistencies of these recommendations, Congress, as part of the Omnibus Anti-Substance Abuse Act of 1988 (Title X), directed the National

Academy of Sciences to determine the level of the BAC whereby an individual will be considered impaired while driving a vehicle. This is a direct acknowledgment of the complexity of the task of establishing these types of levels with any degree of confidence. It also provides recognition that many scientific disciplines such as analytical chemistry, pharmacolgy, biostatistics, and medicine must be involved to reach a clear and rational conclusion as to the appropriate level at which impairment occurs.

Testing of Human Hair for Drugs of Abuse

Hair analysis, primarily to detect opiate abuse, is a newly developing field generating considerable interest for its potential.[18] The uniqueness of hair analysis lies in its promise: Because drugs and/or drug metabolites are deposited within the hair follicle as each hair grows from the scalp, each human hair strand can provide a historical record of an individual's drug use. Hair is known to grow at a fairly constant rate of 1 cm/month, and this suggests that at least theoretically, drug concentration along the hair shaft reflects the level of drug exposure. The distance from the strand of hair being tested to the root serves as the measure of time from drug exposure. The beard may be used for analysis as well, as it has been shown to grow at a rate similar to head hair.

Drugs of abuse which have been detected in hair include the opiates, cocaine, phencyclidine, methamphetamine, nicotine, and phenobarbital. Immunoassays are currently the testing methodology employed, and GC/MS is used for confirmatory testing. However, more controlled studies need to be done in this field because of unresolved validity issues of whether a dose-response relationship exists between administered dose and hair drug levels, and the time course of drug appearance in the hair. Many factors potentially limit validity, including rate of hair growth, drug excretion rates, and environmental contamination. All of these considerations remain as limitations to hair analysis, at least for the present time.

Additional Testing Methods for Drugs of Abuse

Testing for drugs of abuse has hardly been limited to blood, urine, and hair. A simple saliva test for the estimation of blood alcohol levels is already being marketed and used in selected hospital and drug treatment programs.[19] And the forensic science literature has long reported on detecting various drugs in plasma, blood stains, semen, saliva, and perspiration.[20]

Driven by the increasing prevalence of infants being born to drug-dependent mothers and the need to identify those infants as soon as possible after birth, hospital neonatal units have begun to analyze the meconium specimens of newborns. The meconium is the first three days' stool excreted by newborn infants. Early studies appear promising. In paired urine and meconium specimens, there is a higher concentration of drug metabolites in the meconium. The analysis is done by radioimmunoassay for the metabolites of the three commonly abused drugs (heroin, cocaine, and cannabinoids).[21]

TESTING PROCEDURES

Because substance abuse testing methods differ in validity, reliability, and cost, most laboratories today use a system of two tests. These are the initial screening test and the confirmatory test. Also, any analysis of test procedures must recognize that there are a number of equally important components to the testing system: clear and defined drug testing policies and procedures, the testing assay kits themselves, the chain of custody, and the skill and experience of the technicians performing the tests. No part of the system is more critical than the other.

Employers need to have some understanding of the drug testing field in order to make clear, rational personnel policy choices within it. The discussion that follows will present not only the lay terms in common usage, but the technical terms as well.[22]

Sensitivity and Selectivity

Sensitivity means the ability of a test to detect the presence of a compound or chemical in the substance being tested. A test with high sensitivity is capable of detecting minute quantities. *Selectivity* means the ability of a test to discriminate between one compound or chemical and others which are similar. An example of the relationship between sensitivity and selectivity can be shown by discussing the blood test known as VDRL. The VDRL is run routinely on all hospital admissions (and other screenings such as for marriage licenses) to detect syphilis. However, the VDRL will frequently result in a positive finding not because syphilis is present, but rather due to other conditions which can bring about a positive reading (lupus erythematosis, protein abnormalities, and pregnancy). Following a positive result, a more specific test must be done to rule out the false positive results and to confirm the disease if it indeed is present.

Initial and Confirmatory Tests

Because tests have differential sensitivity and selectivity, employers utilize two types of tests to determine the nature and extent of an individual's substance abuse. *The initial test* simply seeks to detect drugs in the urine sample. A common practice has evolved to use initial and screening tests as synonymous terms, but in medical practice there is a clear distinction. Screening tests are highly sensitive, which results in some sacrifice of specificity. This means that a test will show a positive result without detecting the specific drug that is being sought.

In other words, no matter how sensitive a test may be, it cannot override the need for a significant amount of specificity as well. As noted above, high sensitivity without adequate specificity can be the cause of an individual's being identified as positive for taking a drug that is not the one under consideration. This supports the requirement that the initial test *must* be both sensitive and specific for the drug or drug class being sought for identification.

The *confirmatory* test is done to bring the certainty of the initial findings to as close to 100 percent as possible. However, this path is not simple and direct. Rather, it is marked by pitfalls which in many instances are as great as those encountered in the initial testing. The confirmatory test may include just repeating the initial test, which does increase reliability by decreasing the chance that there has been random error in the initial outcome. In most cases, however, the confirmatory test is a more sophisticated and expensive procedure. But again this is not a total guarantee that it will be free from error. It is an essential requirement that the confirmatory test be at least as sensitive and as specific as the initial test.

An important point to clarify is that the system of using two tests *is not* based upon the fact that the initial test is inaccurate. The principles of accuracy must be distinguished from those of reliability and degree of confidence. The degree of confidence can be increased by the two-test system with the finding of a positive result. Yet there may be no improvement in the level of accuracy that is achieved by the initial test alone. Quite obviously when one tests the same item using two different tools of measurement and obtains the same results, the degree of confidence is increased more than if one test were performed, even though the single test may have been as accurate as both tests taken together.

It is important to note as well that the ability to confirm the positive finding on the initial test is limited if the confirmatory test is performed by a completely different method than the initial test. It is possible, therefore, that the confirmatory test may result in a negative finding when in fact the drug is present as has been noted by the initial test. This can occur due to a multitude of variables, among them the skill of the technician performing the test, the test used, and the preestablished cutoff levels.

False Positive and False Negative Test Results

False positive results are a type of testing error wherein a drug or drug metabolite is reported to be present in the sample when in fact it is not. The concept of proficiency tests can assist in making this definition more technically accurate. Proficiency test samples are used for quality control in laboratories and the amount of drug contained in the samples is known exactly. For technical and scientific accuracy, then, using the proficiency model, three types of false positive errors can result: (1) the laboratory test, either initial, confirmatory, or both indicates the presence of a drug when there is none; (2) one or more of a group of chemically related drugs is present in the initial sample but the confirmatory test identifies incorrectly another member of the drug group (this occurs, for example, with the opiates, where morphine may be present in the initial sample but the confirmatory test identifies codeine instead; and (3) a clerical error is at fault.

False negative results are the reverse of the above. The laboratory finds a sample to be free of a drug or drug metabolite but its presence is known to exist. This again is based upon the proficiency model for scientific accuracy, and three types of errors are possible: (1) the laboratory test, either initial, confirmatory, or both indicates the absence of a drug or drug metabolite (based upon established cutoff limits), when in fact the drug is present; (2) the drug is present, but in spite of testing is not found to be present because the cutoff level is higher than that occurring in the sample; and (3) a clerical error occurs.

By now it is readily apparent that testing methodologies are a complex matter involving a high level of scientific technology. But the responsible employer must have the ability to evaluate the drug testing literature for guidelines to validity and reliability before initiating a testing program. Absolutely essential to the discussion of methodology is the principle of cutoffs, yet it probably is the least understood by administrators of drug testing programs.

By definition, the cutoff level for a drug is a value that has been established for the immunoassays by its manufacturer. While this appears to be a straightforward and relatively simple matter, it is not. In reality (defined in both scientific and common-sense terms), the drug is either in the sample or it is not. But the detection of a drug is dependent upon the sensitivity of the test being used. A true positive will give a positive result above the sensitivity level for the test, but it will give a false negative if the drug is present below the sensitivity level.

An additional difficulty may be encountered when a test is so sensitive that the presence of extremely low levels of a drug or drug metabolites will result in a false positive test result. One example of this danger is passive inhalation of marijuana resulting in a positive test result. But recent studies indicate that this is highly unlikely. One study describes a small, unventilated room where several marijuana cigarettes were being smoked at once. The passive parties did not reach a urine concentration above 6ng/ml performed by the GC/MS. The federally mandated and commonly used cutoff is 100ng/ml.[23]

The ingestion of herbal teas brewed from the coca leaf can cause concentrations of cocaine metabolites sufficient to produce positive results. A product known as "Health Inca Tea" has been identified as actually containing enough cocaine to result in a positive test for the cocaine metabolite. The Drug Enforcement Agency (DEA) has since stopped the sale of the product in this country.[24]

Administrative versus Chemical Positives

These difficulties have led to the development of the concepts of "administrative" versus "chemical" positives. Administrators' recognition of the danger of false positives leads to the administrative establishment of a cutoff at a much higher level than the absolute lower limits of the technology's ability to actually detect the drug in a specimen.

Taken together, these factors mean that the cutoff value for reporting positive test results is arbitrary, being established by the manufacturer, the tester, and/or the program administrator. This becomes the "administrative decision" or "administrative positive" and may be in reality different than the "chemical positive." In the laboratory situation this translates to the finding of positive when the sample indicates that the amount of the drug contained in the sample equals or exceeds that of the cutoff calibrator. The finding is said to be negative when there is less drug in the sample than in the cutoff calibrator. There are instances where the sample contains detectable drug(s) which lie between the negative calibrator and the cutoff calibrator. In this situation, the result is read as negative, though the sample probably does contain some of the drug. For statistical certainty, however, in a positive sample, a positive result only occurs above the cutoff calibrator.[25]

There has been much public discussion of the possibility that individuals might be able to adulterate their urine samples in order to avoid a positive finding. Substances which have been identified as possible adulterants include bleach, furniture polish, salt, and water-purification tablets. In addition, some individuals have sought to dilute their urine either by ingesting huge amounts of fluids or by adding water directly to the samples.

It is unlikely that these strategies are effective. In the laboratory situation, the addition of many of these adulterants will result in dramatically abnormal instrumentation readings which will lead to the ready conclusion that there has been an attempt at adulteration. Water loading can result in a lowered concentration of metabolites and false negative test result, but this must be highly calculated by the individual, as timing is critical in urine concentration. And water loading is ineffective if drug concentrations which are high to begin with.

In reality, the drug testing guidelines which have been developed for federal programs appear to be able to essentially eliminate the practice of adding various dilutents to urine samples. Testers restrict access to faucets and add bluing agents to toilets. Additional safeguards include testing urine specific gravity as well as measuring the temperature of the urine immediately upon collection.

There remains a genuine problem with the cross-reactivity with amphetamine-like compunds which can come about when an individual is taking cold medications, allergy medications, and so on. Problems also do arise when individuals consume poppy seeds, which contain both morphine and codeine. A brief history of food and medically used drugs taken just prior to testing can serve to avoid problems in evaluating the legitimacy of positive results.

Quantification and Impairment

The final principle for discussion under urine testing for drugs of abuse is that of quantification. Experts in the drug testing field would like to establish a relationship between drug levels and physiological (mental and physical) impairment similar to that which has been established by the analysis of alcohol blood levels. To date, however, there has been little relationship established between levels of drugs of abuse in the blood and physical impairment. Nor is there an established relationship of drug concentrations in the urine to physical impairment.[26]

SELECTING A DRUG TESTING LABORATORY

The Department of Defense admitted in 1984 that in tests of sixty thousand soldiers about half the urine samples had been mishandled.[27] And one recent court case includes testimony by an employee that he saw a lab technician inadvertently switch labels before placing them on filled sample bottles.[28]

In the period between 1973 and 1981, the national Centers for Disease Control conducted a blind study sending pretested samples to fifty-three laboratories, constituting 12 percent of the total laboratories involved in the CDC program for methadone treatment centers. The results revealed that some labs consistently reported false positives, some as high as 66 percent of the time![29]

Problems such as these are inevitable, given the infancy of the substance abuse testing industry and the amount of money to be made in it. One source reports that in 1985 the drug-test manufacturing industry had worldwide sales totaling $73 billion![30]

To prevent these problems, persons responsible for the design of a substance abuse testing program should be aware that the choice of a laboratory is the most critical one they will make (other than the policy issues which will be discussed in the next chapter). Because the laboratory will be an outside contractor performing specified services for the employer, the personnel director should clearly and carefully specify the criteria for evaluating its performance.

Cost is never the most important criterion. Most laboratories offer to conduct tests for a relatively low amount, particularly if they are also affiliated with a medical facility which offers employee assistance program services on a contract basis to employers to rehabilitate employees who test positive. Obviously, there is more money to be made in treatment than in testing, so contract proposals must be evaluated as to both the quality of the testing program and the quality and cost of treatment programs if these are to be performed by related organizations.

The integrity of the testing process should be ensured by requiring contractors to comply with appropriate standards in four areas: collection, handling, testing, and storage. The National Institute on Drug Abuse has issued voluntary accreditation standards for drug testing laboratories.[31] But the General Accounting Office reports that states differ widely in the extent to which they regulate laboratories in general or drug testing laboratories in particular.[32] For example, only eleven states have specific statutes and regulations that govern laboratories doing employee substance abuse testing: Connecticut, Iowa, Kansas, Maine, Maryland, Minnesota, Nebraska, New York, Oregon, Rhode Island, and Vermont. Because certification criteria and requirements are in such an embryonic stage of development, it is therefore necessary that employers be vigilant in evaluating laboratories before contracting for substance abuse testing services.

Collection

The laboratory should take precautions to ensure that the specimen has not been adulterated by the person providing the sample. This may mean that employees be required to remove all clothing prior to entering the room in which the sample is given so that it is not possible for them to conceal a "clean" sample on their person, that this room be free of places where a "clean" sample could be hidden in advance, and that no sources of water or chemicals (such as sinks or toilets) be available as source of possible adulterants to the sample.

Handling

Once the sample has been collected, it should be sealed to prevent tampering and immediately labeled to provide foolproof identification. Collected samples should be handled so as to prevent loss, damage, or substitution in shipment and testing.

Testing

Split-sample techniques should be used to ensure test validity and reliability. That is, a collected sample should be divided into three parts upon arrival at the laboratory. One part should be tested initially, a second part should be used for the confirmatory test if the first test is positive, and the third part should be frozen for future use as evidence in court (if the test results are used as the basis for disciplinary action or discharge and the employee sues as a result).

Laboratory personnel should possess the qualifications and certifications required to perform tests appropriately and accurately. Technicians should be certified by whatever federal or state agency has jurisdiction over the laboratory. Test results should be read, interpreted, and reported only by those qualified to do so. Positive results should be reported only to the appropriate person in the company or agency, and this reporting should take place only after positive results of an initial screening have been confirmed. The laboratory will base positive determinations on appropriate cutoff levels established by the employer, by federal regulations, or other standards agreed upon in advance.

Storage

Once collected and tested, samples should be stored so as to permit their retrieval and use as evidence should this be necessary to justify personnel actions by the employer.

Choosing a Testing Laboratory

The choice of a testing laboratory is the most important decision the personnel director can make to ensure that testing is done well. Two frequently cited surveys evaluated the accuracy and reliability of drug testing in laboratories. The first was done by the Centers for Disease Control (CDC) and involved thirteen laboratories in which each received 100 samples from the CDC proficiency program. The error rates reported were 37 percent to 69 percent.[33] While the study is often cited to

Table 5
Blind Proficiency Testing Programs

Sample Results	Number
Dept. of Defense 1983–1987:	
Negative	
Number tested	48,886
Number correctly identified	48,886
False positive rate (%)	0.0
Positive	
Number tested	25,523
Number correctly identified	24,483
False negative rate (%)	4.1
U.S. Coast Guard 1983–1988:	
Negative	
Number tested	10,450
Number correctly identified	10,450
False positive rate (%)	0.0
Positive	
Number tested	2,511
Number correctly identified	2,433
False negative rate (%)	3.1

support those who question the ability of laboratories to provide drug testing in an accurate and reliable manner, those who claim high levels of laboratory performance cite several important points regarding the study. The errors that were reported were false negatives for the most part. This may well have been due to the cutoff being set too high to detect the drug even when it was actually present. False positive results, on the other hand, were as low as 0–3 percent for most drugs. Probably the most significant point of this critique is that the error rates were found only on single tests, because there was no confirmation testing done. Supporters claim that this study cannot be considered representative of modern testing laboratory methods using the two-test system of initial and confirmation testing. As one researcher states,

> If the principles of selection of a good laboratory that is monitored by blind proficiency testing are followed and if positive screening test results are confirmed by gas chromatography/mass spectrometry, no analytic false positives should occur.[34]

The American Association for Clinical Chemistry (AACC) conducted the second survey of drug testing laboratories which documented the validity of their findings. In this study, 1,880 samples were submitted to forty-seven laboratories. The findings were only fourteen (0.8 percent) false negatives and one false positive (0.05 percent).[35]

Probably the best support that laboratories can indeed perform in a highly accurate manner is to note the results of the blind proficiency testing program for military laboratories, which is administered by the Armed Forces Institute of Pathology (AFIP). Table 5 is a summary of results from the AFIP program from 1983–1987. Coast Guard data is also given for the years 1983–1988. Out of a total sample of 59,336 known to be free of drugs, not one false positive test was found. On samples totaling 28,034 in which one or more drugs were present, the false negative rate was between 3 percent and 4 percent.[36]

SUMMARY

Substance abuse testing originated with psychiatric investigations of alcohol abuse. The application of these techniques to workplace drug testing requires that human resource managers understand the strengths, weaknesses, and terminology of the laboratory testing process.

The cheapest, easiest, and perhaps most valid substance abuse testing techniques involve the collection of data through interviews and questionnaires. If laboratory testing methods are used, the employer should carefully select a testing laboratory that follows accepted NIDA procedures with respect to collection, testing, handling, and storage of samples. Human resource managers should be aware that laboratory testing techniques cannot be assumed to be valid and reliable. They must accept that cutoff levels for determining whether an employee tests positive are not objective. Rather, they reflect a combination of factors—administrative judgments, the sensitivity and selectivity of the test, and the skill of the technician who analyzes the sample.

NOTES

1. Weiss, C., & Millman, R. (1989). Alcohol and drug abuse in the workplace in broad perspective. *Bulletin New York Academy of Medicine, 65*, pp. 173–184.

2. Ibid.

3. Sobell, L., & Sobell, M. (1975). Outpatient alcoholics give valid self-reports. *Journal of Nervous and Mental Diseases, 161*, pp. 32–42.

4. Cyr, M., & Wartman, S. (1988). The effectiveness of routine screening questions in the detection of alcoholism. *Journal of the American Medical Association, 259*, pp. 51–54.

5. Persson, J., & Magnusson, P. (1988). Comparison between different methods of detecting patients with excessive consumption of alcohol. *Acta Medicine Scandinavian, 223*, pp. 101–109.

6. Hurt, R., Morse, R., & Swenson, W. (1980). Diagnosis of alcoholism with a self-administered alcoholism screening test: Results with 1,002 consecutive patients receiving general examinations. *Mayo Clinical Procedures, 55*, pp. 365–370.

7. Pokorny, A., Miller, B., & Kaplan, H. (1972). The brief MAST: A shortened version of the Michigan alcoholism screening test (MAST). *American Journal of Psychiatry, 129*, pp. 342–345.

8. Bush, B., Shaw, S., Cleary, P., Delbanco, T., & Aronson, M. (1987). Screening for alcohol abuse using the CAGE questionnaiare. *American Journal of Medicine, 82*, pp. 231–235.

9. McClellan, A., Luborsky, L., Woody, G., & O'Brien, C. (1980). An improved diagnostic evaluation instrument for substance abuse patients. *Journal of Nervous and Mental Disease, 168*, pp. 28–33.

10. Chick, J., Kreitman, N., & Plant, M. (1981). Mean cell volume and gamma-glutamyl-transpeptidase as markers of drinking in working men. *Lancet, 1*, pp. 1249–1251.

11. VuDuc, T. (1987). Additional results in the validation of the bond elut-THC extraction column-TLC as a confirmation method for EMIT and RIA-positive cannabinoid urines. *Journal of Analytic Toxicology, 11*, p. 83.

12. Hawks, R. (1986). Urine testing for drugs of abuse. *NIDA research monograph 73*. Washington, D.C.: Department of Health and Human Services, pp. 30–53.

13. Finkle, B. (1987). Drug analysis technology: Overview and state of the art. *Clinical Chemistry, 33* (11B), pp. 138–178.

14. McCunny, R. (1989). Drug testing: Technical complications of a complex social issue. *American Journal of Industrial Medicine, 15*, pp. 601–605.

15. Dubowski, K. (1985). Absorption, distribution, and elimination of alcohol: Highway safety aspects. *Journal of Studies of Alcohol* (suppl.), *10*, pp. 98–108.

16. Dubowski, K. (1982). Alcohol analysis: Clinical laboratory aspects, part I. *Laboratory Management, 20*, pp. 43–54.

17. Mitchell, M. (1985). Alcohol induced impairment of central nervous system function: Behavioral skills involved in driving. *Journal of Studies of Alcohol* (suppl.), *10*, pp. 109–116.

18. Baumgartner, A., Jones, P., Baumgartner, W., & Black, C. (1979). Radioimmunoassay of hair for determining opiate-abuse histories. *Journal of Nuclear Medicine, 20*, pp. 748–752.

19. Chem-Elec, Inc., of North Webster (Indiana), markets ALCO-Screen, which it describes as a "simple 2-minute saliva test for the estimation of blood alcohol levels."

20. Smith, F., & Pomposini, D. (1981). Detection of phenobarbital in bloodstains, semen, seminal stains, saliva stains, perspiration stains, and hair. *Journal of Forensic Science, 26*(3), pp. 582–586.

21. Ostrea, E., Brady, M., Parks, P., Arsenio, D., & Naluz, A. (1989). Drug screening of meconium in infants of drug-dependent mothers: An alternative to urine testing. *Journal of Pediatrics, 115*, pp. 474–477.

22. Rinaldi, R., Steindler, E., Wilford, B., & Goodwin, D. (1988). Clarification and standardization of substance abuse terminology. *Journal of the American Medical Association, 259*, pp. 555–557.

23. Mule, S., Lomax, P., & Gross, S. (1988). Active and realistic passive marijuana exposure tested by three immunoassays and GC/MS in urine. *Journal of Analytic Toxicology, 12*, pp. 113–116.

24. Siegel, R., El-Sohly, M., Plowman, T., Rury, P., & Jones, R. (1986). Cocaine in herbal tea (letter). *Journal of the American Medical Association, 255*, p. 40.

25. Hawks, R. (1986). Urine testing for drugs of abuse. *NIDA research monograph 73*. Washington, D.C.: Department of Health and Human Services, pp. 30–53.

26. Drug concentrations and driving impairment. (1985). *Journal of the American Medical Association, 254*, pp. 2818–2831.

27. Castro, B. (1986, March 17). Battling the enemy within. *Time*, p. 56.

28. National Treasury Employees Union, 649 F. Supp. at 390.

29. Hansen, H., Caudill, S., & Boone, J. (1985). Crisis in drug testing: Results of CDC blind study. *Journal of the American Medical Association, 253*, p. 2382.

30. Kasouf, D. (1985, October 15). Booming market for a variety of tests. *Public Administration Times*, p. 1.

31. Accrediting plan set for drug testing labs. (1987, June 1). *Public Administration Times*, p. 1.

32. United States General Accounting Office. (1988). *Employee Drug Testing: Regulation of Drug Testing Laboratories*. Washington, D.C.: U.S.G.A.O., GAO/GGD-88-127FS.

33. Hansen, H., Caudill, S., & Boone, J. Crisis in drug testing. *Journal of the American Medical Association, 253*, pp. 2382–2387.

34. Boone, D. (1987). Reliability of urine testing. *Journal of the American Medical Association, 258*, p. 2587.

35. Finge, C., White, R., & Battaglia, D. (1987). Status of drugs of abuse testing in urine: An AACC study. *Clinical Chemistry, 33*, 1683–1686.

36. Quality reports on blind sample proficiency testing: 1983–87. (1989). Washington, D.C.: Department of Defense Detection Quality Control Laboratory, Armed Forces Institute of Pathology.

3

Substance Abuse Testing and the Law

Drug testing is an invasive procedure which may lead to an applicant's being denied employment, or to the discipline and discharge of an employee who is otherwise performing satisfactorily. Therefore, testing in the public sector raises critical constitutional issues about employees' right to privacy and due process. The private sector is freer to implement testing programs because it is not required to conduct personnel practices so as to protect employees' constitutional rights. However, courts have determined that some significant restrictions apply to the ways in which private employers may test and the uses they may make of the results. And both public- and private-sector employees are bound by the provisions of civil rights and handicap protection laws.

OBJECTIVES

The purpose of this chapter is to:

1. Describe the ways in which constitutional protections against invasion of privacy and violation of due process affect substance abuse testing policies and procedures in public agencies.

2. Compare these legal constraints with those which apply to private sector employers.

3. Discuss the provisions of the Drug Free Workplace Act which apply to federal government agencies and federal contractors.

4. Discuss and evaluate the civil rights and handicap protection laws affecting both public- and private-sector employers.

PUBLIC SECTOR

Substance abuse testing by public employers has traditionally been circumscribed by constitutional protections. The Fourth Amendment provides that

The right of the people to be secure in their persons, houses, papers, and effects, against unreasonable searches and seizures, shall not be violated, and no warrants shall issue, but upon probable cause, supported by oath or affirmation, and particularly describing the place to be searched, and the person or thing to be seized.

Blood and urine tests easily qualify as "searches" under the Fourth Amendment. And historically persons (including employees) were protected against "unreasonable" searches by the requirement that the employer show individualized suspicion ("just cause" that the employee was a substance abuser, such as a critical performance incident or substance impairment).[1]

But public and political pressures in recent years have increased the relative importance of the public's right to a productive work force over the employees' right to privacy against searches. In 1986, President Reagan signed E.O. 12564, requiring all federal agencies to develop and implement substance abuse testing and employee assistance programs for their employees.[2] Understandably, the critical policy issues were the extent to which the employer was required to show reasonable suspicion prior to testing and the criteria for determining whether a position is "sensitive" or not.

In 1989 (*National Treasury Employees Union* v. *Von Raab*), the Supreme Court approved the program of the U.S. Customs Service to test certain of its employees who carry firearms, who are involved in the interdiction of illegal drugs, or who have access to classified information—*regardless of whether individualized suspicion could be shown prior to testing.*[3] The case was decided on a 5-4 vote, with the majority opinion written by Justice Arthur Kennedy.[4] The majority believed that

in light of the extraordinary safety and national security hazards that would attend the promotion of drug users to positions that require the carrying of firearms or interdiction of controlled substances, the Service's policy of deterring drug users from seeking such promotions cannot be deemed unreasonable.

This was particularly true given that

the Customs Service is our Nation's first line of defense against one of the greatest problems affecting the health and welfare of our population.

The majority believed that

the government has a compelling interest in ensuring that front-line interdiction personnel are physically fit, and have unimpeachable integrity and judgment.

But Justice Antonin Scalia, writing the minority opinion, concluded that the service had not presented evidence adequate to document the existence of a drug problem. Therefore, he dissented by expressing concern that by extending drug testing to employees who carry firearms, the majority opinion would subject a large number of public employees "to this needless indignity." He stated that if those who carry guns can be tested for drugs, then

so can all others whose work, if performed under the influence of drugs, may endanger others—automobile drivers, operators of other potentially dangerous equipment, construction workers, school crossing guards.

The majority and dissenting opinions are both clear statements of opposing viewpoints. Given the close nature of the vote in this case, it remains to be seen how other federal courts will resolve future substance abuse testing cases so as to balance these competing legitimate needs to control substance abuse among employees who occupy sensitive positions related to public health and safety, and employee rights to privacy in the absence of prior knowledge that a substance abuse problem exists.

State and local governments may also have laws regulating substance abuse testing for public agencies and their employees.[5]

PRIVATE SECTOR

The critical distinction between private- and public-sector employers is that the private sector is not bound by constitutional restrictions against violation of privacy and due process.

Constitutional rights restrict the actions of federal, state and local governmental entities only, and thus the actions of private employers in drug-testing cases ordinarily escape constitutional scrutiny.[6]

However, federal courts have long held that in some situations the activities of the private employer are so close to those of the government that the limitations normally applied to government are also applied to the private sector. In the most recent case law available, the Supreme Court has provided a four-part test to determine whether the activities of a private employer (such as a substance abuse testing program) meet this "state action" requirement:

> (1) whether the income of the private employer is derived from government funding, (2) whether state regulation of the private employer is extensive and detailed, (3) whether the function performed by the private employer is traditionally the exclusive prerogative of the state, and (4) whether a symbiotic relationship between the private employer and the state exists.[7]

In *Samuel Skinner, Secretary of Transportation* v. *Railway Labor Executives' Association*, the Supreme Court voted 7-2 in 1989 to uphold federal regulations that required railway employees who were involved in certain serious train accidents to be tested, and permitted the testing of those who violated safety rules or were suspected to be impaired because of drug abuse.

The Federal Railway Administration (FRA) had issued regulations mandating blood and urine tests of train crews that were involved in a major train accident, an impact accident which resulted in a reportable injury or damage to railroad property of at least $50,000, or an incident that involved a fatality to a railroad employee. The Railway Labor Executives' Association (representing engineers, brakemen, and other railroad employees) filed a lawsuit challenging the constitutionality of these regulations. The District Court ruled in favor of the FRA, but the U.S. Court of Appeals for the Ninth Circuit reversed since it believed that individualized suspicion was necessary prior to requiring employees to submit to blood or urine testing.

Citing evidence that substance abuse was apparently a problem among railroad employees, the Supreme Court upheld the regulations by concluding that "the government interest in testing without a showing of individualized suspicion is compelling."[8] The majority concluded that the railroad industry was already pervasively regulated to ensure safety, and that safety was in part dependent upon the health and fitness of covered employees. Also, it considered it likely that employees could cause serious damage before any evidence of impairment became evident to supervisors or others.

Therefore, given that substance abuse testing would function both as a check on employee substance abuse and a protection of the public welfare, the Court concluded that

> the toxicological testing contemplated by the regulations is not an undue infringement on the justifiable expectations of privacy of covered employees, [and that] . . . it would be unrealistic, and inimicable to the Govern-

ment's goal of ensuring safety in rail transportation, to require a showing of individualized suspicion in these circumstances.

The Court's subsequent actions (in the 1990 term) confirm that it is not likely to decide another substance abuse testing case in the near future. The Court declined to review two substance abuse testing cases (*National Federation of Federal Employees* v. *Richard Cheney, Secretary of Defense*, Docket No. 89-635, and *Daniel Bell* v. *Richard Thornburgh, Attorney General of the United States*, Docket No. 89-679) which upheld substance abuse testing programs of the Department of the Army and the Department of Justice. In the latter case, this refusal to review has the effect of reiterating the policies enunciated in *National Treasury Employees Union* v. *Von Raab*: that is, issues of security and public welfare will tend to predominate over the privacy rights of federal employees. In *Daniel Bell* v. *Richard Thornburgh, Attorney General of the United States*, the Court's refusal to review had the effect of upholding the policies it enunciated in *Samuel Skinner, Secretary of Transportation* v. *Railway Labor Executives' Association*: the great threat to public welfare caused by substance abuse among employees of closely regulated private employers (in this case civilian police, guards, and individuals who fly and service aircraft), and the usefulness of substance abuse testing as a check on employee substance abuse, means that random testing of these employees is not an unreasonable infringement on their privacy.[9]

Other legal arguments which may protect private sector employees against substance abuse testing are:

- State labor laws or municipal ordinances (such as in San Francisco) may prohibit mandatory substance abuse testing,[10] just as such laws may prohibit or regulate polygraph testing.[11] And where substance abuse testing is not prohibited, it can be tightly regulated—at least a dozen states have relevant statutes, which vary widely.[12]
- The "implied covenant of good faith and fair dealing," a court-created contract right between the employer and employee, could be used by a court to strike down random or for-cause testing of employees.[13]

These considerations mean that substance abuse testing is a legally uncertain process for private sector employers as well. While there are no constitutional protections against violation of privacy rights, the concepts of "state action" and contractual employment rights do serve as limits to the legality of wholesale testing without cause.[14]

THE FEDERAL AGENCY DRUG-FREE WORKPLACE ACT OF 1988

The Federal Agency Drug-Free Workplace Act of 1988 affects companies that signed federal contracts worth more than $25,000 on or after March 18, 1989, as well as companies that seek to renew expiring contracts or accept new work orders under ongoing contracts that predated the law's effective date. Under the act, employers must provide each worker with a statement notifying him or her that the unlawful manufacture, distribution, dispensing, possession, or use of illegal drugs is prohibited in that workplace, and specifying the actions that will be taken against violators. An employee will not be allowed to work on the federal contract unless he or she agrees to comply with the statement and to notify the employer of any drug convictions. Failure to meet the law's requirements could result in suspension or termination of the federal contract or could prevent the company from contracting with the U.S. government for up to five years.

HANDICAP PROTECTION

The Rehabilitation Act of 1973, which applies to federal agencies or recipients of federal funds, states that applicants and employees who are substance abusers are not normally considered handicapped within the meaning of federal statutes.[15] But prior substance abusers or those whose current use would not impair their performance or threaten the property or safety of others are considered to be handicapped for purposes of this statute.

Employees who voluntarily seek help from their employer for a substance abuse problem are protected from disciplinary action or termination as long as they are undergoing treatment. Following treatment, they are entitled to retain their prior position (sometimes upon condition of submitting to random substance abuse tests). If this position is considered "sensitive" or high-risk, they may be entitled to another position within the organization if one is available.

Prior to taking disciplinary action based on a substance abuse test result, employers covered by this law should attempt to determine that an employee who tests positive constitutes a threat to the safety of either other employees or the public and that alternative positions are not available. This will help to mitigate any potential claim that the individual is a handicapped person entitled to the protections afforded by this law.

SUMMARY

Substance abuse testing is a "search" of the employee's body. It is so invasive and degrading that it should never be undertaken unless it can be demonstrated that the sensitive nature of the position is so clear, or the risk to the public welfare that would result from impairment is so great, as to override the employee's right to privacy and the presumption that individualized suspicion is necessary before the search is authorized.

NOTES

1. Annas, G. (1989, May-June). Crack, symbolism and the Constitution. *Hastings Center Report*, pp. 35–37; Neisser, E. (1986, October 23). Job tests, not urine tests. *New Jersey*

Law Journal, p. 6; Stern, K. (1986). Government drug testing and individual privacy rights: Crying wolf in the workplace. *Yale Law & Policy Review, 5*, pp. 235–259; Miller, D. (1986). Mandatory urinalysis testing and the privacy rights of subject employees: Toward a general rule of legality under the Fourth Amendment. *University of Pittsburgh Law Review, 48*, pp. 201–245; and Curran, W. (1987, February). Compulsory drug testing: The legal barriers. *The New England Journal of Medicine, 316*(6), pp. 318–321.

2. Executive Order 12564. (1986, September 15); implemented by FPM Letter 792-16, Establishing a drug-free federal workplace, U.S. Office of Personnel Management, November 28, 1986.

3. Stuart, P. (1989, August). Keeping your work place drug free. *Business & Health*, p. 55.

4. National Treasury Employees v. William Von Raab, Commissioner, United States Customs Service (Docket 86-1879).

5. Reichenberg, N. (1988). *Drug testing in the workplace*. Alexandria, VA: International Personnel Management Association, pp. 9–15.

6. Fogel, S., Kornblut, G., & Porter, N. Survey of the law on employee drug testing. (1988, January). *University of Miami Law Review, 42*, p. 567.

7. Fogel, S., Kornblut, G., & Porter, N. Survey of the law on employee drug testing. (1988, January). *University of Miami Law Review, 42*, p. 553, citing *Rendell-Baker* at 840–843.

8. Samuel Skinner, Secretary of Transportation v. Railway Labor Executives' Association (Docket No. 87-1555).

9. Supreme Court declines review of drug testing cases. (1990, March). *IPMA News*, p. 7.

10. San Francisco Municipal Ordinance No. 527-85. (1985, November 18). Employee activities and drug testing, File No. 97-85-44.

11. Burkett, J., & Feldman, H. (1979). *The detection of deception: A lie detection operations manual*. New Jersey: Allison Press.

12. Green, W. (1989, November 21). Drug testing becomes a corporate mine field. *The Wall Street Journal*, pp. B1, B9; and Beissert, W. (1987, March 24). Drug-testing guidelines are considered by states. *USA Today*, p. 1.

13. Richman, D. (1986, November 7). Legal uncertainties complicate hospitals' testing for drug abuse. *Modern Health Care, 16*(23), p. 148.

14. Susser, P. (1985, January). Legal issues raised by drugs in the workplace. *Labor Law Journal, 36*(1), pp. 42–54; Unrestricted private employee drug testing programs: An invasion of the worker's right to privacy. (1986). *California Western Law Review, 23*, pp. 72–94; and Hartsfield, W. (1986, October). Medical examinations as a method of investigating employee wrongdoing. *Labor Law Journal*, pp. 692–702.

15. Reichenberg, N. (1988). *Drug testing in the workplace*. Alexandria, VA: International Personnel Management Association, p. 4.

4

Personnel Policies and Practices

Drug and alcohol abuse is a tremendous problem in our society from a legal, economic, social, medical, political, and managerial perspective.[1] Liability risks, economic costs, and demands for high productivity have led many employers to initiate drug and alcohol screening programs. Yet substance abuse testing is not a cure-all. First, all of the tests raise issues of validity and reliability. Second, particularly in the public sector, issues of privacy and due process may restrict the employer's right to collect and use substance abuse screening data to discipline or discharge employees. And most importantly, no substance abuse testing should be conducted unless clear policies and procedures have first been developed. The employer should make every effort to gain employees' cooperation. This means orienting employees and training supervisors so that the policies that are carried out are the same ones that were developed. Everyone must be clear from the start on who is to be tested, and under what circumstances. And what will be done with the results?

OBJECTIVES

The purposes of this chapter are to:

1. Describe the substance abuse testing policies and procedures now used by public agencies and private companies throughout the United States.
2. Summarize the critical questions any workplace substance abuse policy must answer if it is to be clear, effective, well received by employees, and legally defensible. (A model substance abuse testing policy which employers may wish to use or adapt for their own workplace is given in Appendix A.)
3. For private sector employers, to summarize the problems with testing from a technical, legal, and human relations perspective, and provide alternatives to testing for those employers who choose not to implement it.
4. For public agency employers, to evaluate the implications of these policies and programs for three critical public policy concerns—public employees' right to protection against violations of their constitutional rights to privacy and due process, elected officials' demands for enforcement of the public's right to an effective public service, and management's need to mitigate the effects of employee substance abuse in order to reduce liability risks and increase program effectiveness.

WHAT SUBSTANCE ABUSE TESTING POLICIES DO EMPLOYERS NOW USE?

Private Sector

Briefly stated, major employers throughout the United States have responded to the problem of substance abuse by agreeing that a substance-abuse-free workplace is desirable. Most employers have moved to create this by testing all applicants, and also employees under some conditions.

In the private sector, employers are much more able to implement testing procedures, since these employers to not have to fulfill the stricter constitutional standards to which the public employer is held.[2] The number of companies testing applicants or employees for substance abuse increased from 5 percent in 1982 to 40 percent in 1987. According to the Department of Labor, 20 percent of all American workers are now employed by companies that test for drug use.[3] Testing of applicants rose to 25 percent in 1988.[4]

Public Sector

Substance abuse testing of public sector employees has occurred since 1981. Because there are over 20,000 separate government jurisdictions which have different testing policies, it has been difficult to develop an accurate and comprehensive picture of public agency policies and procedures.

The Clearinghouse on Workplace Drug and AIDS Policy was created in 1986 by the American Society for Public Administration's Section on Personnel Administration and Labor Relations. In 1987–88, the Clearinghouse undertook a comprehensive survey of public agency drug testing policies and procedures, using a sample of 300 personnel directors from public agencies at all levels of government in the United States.[5] The sample is not random. Rather, it is designed to include those jurisdictions which are most likely to be developing managerial responses to the critical public policy issues raised by drug testing. It comprises the fifty states, the 100 largest cities, all counties over 500,000 population, and all federal cabinet-level departments and independent agencies. It was compiled with the help of membership directories provided by the International Personnel Management Association (IPMA) and the National Association of Counties (NACO).

This study is designed to answer a range of questions about how public agencies have responded to demands that they create managerial policies and practices related to substance abuse. Specifically, its objective is to present baseline data which will acquaint public administrators with current policy and practice in this area and guide them in further investigating the relationship of substance abuse testing in the workplace to the human resource management policies and personnel practices of public agencies.[6] The questionnaire employed in this study was designed and used by the IPMA to solicit their individual and organizational members' responses to drug testing.[7]

Here are the results of the survey. Thirty-two percent of the personnel directors consider substance abuse among their employees to be a serious problem. Cities and counties are more likely than other levels of government to do so. Sixty-five percent of these agencies have substance abuse policies in place, or are considering adopting them, 35 percent neither have them in place nor are considering them. Cities and counties are more likely than other levels of government to have testing policies in place. But this difference is disappearing as other levels of government develop testing policies—there is no significant association between level of government and whether a jurisdiction has a policy in place or is considering adopting one. Those governments that view the substance abuse problem as significant are more likely to have a policy in place, or to be developing one.

Sixty-six percent of the governments which have a substance abuse policy in place or who are developing one test applicants. Forty-six percent of all respondents test employees under some circumstances. Cities and counties are more likely than other levels of government to test applicants. Governments which have a substance abuse policy in place or which are adopting one are more likely to test applicants than those without policies. Sixty-three percent of the sixty-seven public agencies which test applicants do so for public safety positions (police and firefighters). Agencies are more likely to test applicants for these positions than for any others.

Sixty-eight percent of those public agencies which test employees do so following performance incidents or upon the supervisor's reasonable suspicion. Public agencies with a policy in place are more likely to refuse employment to applicants who refuse to be tested. However, these agencies are not more likely to know what types of disciplinary action they will take against employees who test positive. Ninety-one percent of those public agencies which test employees verify positive results on the initial test with a second test before taking disciplinary action. Discipline, which includes termination, may vary for 35 percent of the respondents based on the level of concentration (alcohol levels can be measured through blood sample or breathalyzer; the presence of drugs can be detected in urine, but not their level of concentration), 51 percent based on job class, or 50 percent based on prior performance evaluations. Governments with policies in place, or those planning to adopt them, are not more likely to protect applicants' rights by informing them in advance that they will be tested, nor are they more likely to require applicants' written consent.

Eighty-five percent of respondent public agencies have a program to provide employees with counseling and medical help with substance abuse problems. Those governments that have or are contemplating the adoption of an alcohol/drug testing policy are more likely to have an employee asssistance program (EAP). And their EAPs are more likely to assist in evaluation and rehabilitation of referred employees.

Three discriminant variables are statistically significant predictors of whether or not a government has a policy in place or is considering adopting one. They are whether the EAP itself conducts tests, whether the EAP assists in evaluation and rehabilitation, and whether the personnel director perceives the problem as significant.[8, 9]

PUBLIC POLICY ISSUES RELATED TO WORKPLACE SUBSTANCE ABUSE TESTING

It is clear that many employees abuse alcohol and other drugs and that public agencies are heavily involved in substance abuse testing. Then why do so many personnel directors think this is not a serious problem? Why don't they have testing policies in place?

Personnel directors may be unready to develop clear policies toward substance abuse or even unsure how to view it, because they quickly learn that the issue includes tough dilemmas. The primary practical issue is whether rejecting applicants and disciplining employees who test positive is a useful way of stopping employee drug abuse. The primary legal issue is whether personnel policies or practices should distinguish between legal drugs (alcohol and prescription drugs) and illegal ones.[10] And ethically sensitive personnel directors may also wonder if substance abuse has a greater effect on employee job performance than employees' personalities, family problems, debts, mental illness, or other issues. And once managers admit that some employees have a substance abuse problem, the agency is legally and politically bound to do something about it (though the economic costs of treatment and the legal risks of liability may make an "ostrich" approach more attractive to management).

Employees are usually protected by collective bargaining agreements or civil service regulations which make it hard to discipline them. Since applicants have no such rights, it is not surprising that those agencies which admit that a substance abuse problem exists respond to it by testing applicants. But then why do most respondents consider the testing of applicants to be merely a selection criterion (like a physical exam or reference check) rather than a broad area of personnel practice requiring underlying policy direction? Obviously, personnel managers may prefer to use the blood and urine samples already collected in preemployment physicals to detect substance abuse without applicants' knowledge or consent. But this is a poor managerial practice which can lead to lawsuits by applicants.

Most personnel directors report that they do not hire applicants who refuse to be tested. But they also state that under some circumstances they will consider applicants who test positive for future employment. Have agencies in fact hired applicants who previously tested positive, or will they do so in the future? If not, this would result in informal "blacklisting" of applicants and the eventual creation of a two-tier employment market, with the top tier closed to applicants who have ever tested positive for substance abuse.

Agencies who test current employees do so primarily based upon incidents or reasonable suspicion, as defined by the supervisor. But because governments with policies are not more likely to know what to do with employees who test positive than governments without policies, it does not seem that the presence of a testing policy will provide a clearer definition of these terms for supervisors. What the agency does with an employee who tests positive may vary depending on level of concentration, job class, and/or employee performance. Therefore, it does not seem reasonable to expect that supervisors can identify or refer suspected substance-abusing employees skillfully and equitably, particularly in the face of union opposition and due-process protections. Instead, in the absence of clear guidelines and rewards, they are more likely to avoid these risks by declining to identify suspected substance abusers or to refer them for testing and treatment. If substance abuse testing is to work, we must face the issue of how to sell it to supervisors.

Most employers report that they have employee assistance programs (EAPs), and that these assist employees with abuse problems. These are commendable responses. But do we really solve a problem by creating an organizational unit (such as affirmative action, collective bargaining, risk management) and then assigning troublesome problems to it? Given the uncertain adequacy of their location, mission, budget, and objectives, can EAPs provide the quality of testing and rehabilitative services needed to meet this crisis, at a price agencies and their employees can afford?

While many public personnel directors view substance abuse testing of applicants and employees as risky, there is no doubt that it gives them an opportunity to play a critical role in solving the substance abuse crisis. The significance which the personnel director attaches to workplace substance abuse correlates highly with whether the agency has developed policies in this area or is considering doing so. Given that leadership by public personnel managers makes a difference, we must act.[11]

CRITICAL POLICY ISSUES

Given these concerns, it is clear that personnel managers must have clear answers to a range of questions related to workplace substance abuse testing.[12] It is no coincidence that these are the issues at which a court will look when it evaluates the validity of an employer's testing program. These are the questions:

Do you have good reasons for instituting a substance abuse testing program?

- Does your industry have a high accident rate, or is your company's accident rate higher than the industry average?
- Have accidents occurred that may have been drug or alcohol related?
- Have there been measurable changes in productivity over the last few years?
- Is absenteeism higher than normal?
- Is the company paying more medical and hospitalization benefits than before, particularly for psychiatric rehabilitative disorders?
- Are other companies similar to yours instituting testing programs for employees?
- Are they screening job applicants?

Who gets tested when?

- Will you test applicants, or applicants and employees?
- If you test applicants, will you test all applicants, or only those for certain positions?
- If you test all new hires, will you test as part of the application process, or after the job offer but before hiring?
- Do you require a preemployment physical? Is substance abuse testing a routine part of the physical?
- Will you tell applicants that hiring is subject to substance abuse test results? If so, will you tell them when they apply for the job, or just prior to the physical?
- If an applicant tests positive will you bar employment permanently? Will you reconsider the application after a waiting period? If so, how long? Will it depend upon the job for which the applicant is being considered?

- If you eventually hire an applicant who failed the test, will you set any job restrictions to reduce liability risks? Will you require periodic, random testing? Will you inform the supervisor?

- If you test employees, will you test all employees (universally or randomly), or all employees in certain "sensitive" positions; or will you test employees only if there is a decline in performance, a critical incident, or "reasonable suspicion"?

- How will you define "sensitive" positions?

- How will you objectively measure employee performance along previously established standards (job elements)?

- What is a critical incident?

- What constitutes "reasonable suspicion," or "probable cause"?

- Will the judgment as to whether a critical incident, probable cause, or drop in performance has occurred be made by a supervisor? By the personnel department? By a physician?

- What will happen if an employee refuses to be tested? Will he or she be disciplined or terminated for insubordination?

Are the tests conducted according to procedures which are designed to minimize their intrusion into the privacy rights of employees, ensure the accuracy of results, and protect the integrity of collected samples?

- In addition to the standard illegal drugs (cocaine, marijuana) and prescription drugs subject to abuse (amphetamines, barbiturates, tranquilizers) which all labs test for, will you test for alcohol? Will you test for nicotine?

- What precautions will you take to ensure that the specimen has not been adulterated by the person providing the sample?

- How is the sample sealed to prevent tampering?

- How is the sample labeled so as to provide foolproof identification?

- How are collected samples handled so as to prevent loss, damage, or substitution in shipment and testing?

- Are split-sample techniques used to ensure test validity and reliability?

- Are positive samples kept frozen so that they can be used accurately in court if necessary?

- Are laboratory personnel certified technicians?

- Who will read and interpret the test results?

- What type of drug test(s) will you use for initial screening?

- Are positive test results withheld until and unless they are confirmed by a second, more sophisticated test such as the GC/MS?

- What cutoff levels will you use to determine the presence of a substance in a sample?
- How are test results reported to the employer? Hard copy, or verbally?
- Are positive tests reported only to the personnel director, or to others as well (supervisors, top management)? Are they placed in the employee's personnel file?
- Are positive test results reported to anyone outside the organization (the individual's physician, or law enforcement officials)? If so, what do you expect them to do with the information?
- How will you ensure confidentiality of test results?
- Who will tell the employee, and how?
- What will you do with the results?
- Will employees who test positive be disciplined, terminated, reassigned, or rehabilitated? Will this choice depend on other factors such as the employee's seniority, previous performance evaluations or current level of performance, type of position held, or the level of concentration of the substance abused?
- Will terminated employees be eligible for rehire? If so, when and under what circumstances?
- Is your employee assistance program (EAP) run by experienced professionals?
- Do local treatment centers exist which have been evaluated and deemed capable of handling substance abuse rehabilitation?
- If your company supports rehabilitation, who pays for it? To what extent does your insurance coverage include inpatient and outpatient treatment for substance abuse?
- If employees volunteer for treatment by the EAP or voluntarily submit to treatment upon the order of their supervisor, will their jobs be held for them pending completion of treatment and rehabilitation?
- Are they protected against discipline or termination while in the EAP?
- Will the EAP be available for counseling and support following detoxification and rehabilitation?
- Will employees who are rehabilitated be subject to periodic substance abuse testing? To random testing?
- May employees be referred to the EAP only once, or more than once if their substance abuse continues following rehabilitation?

Does the employer in fact conduct all substance abuse testing within these clear, written policies and procedures? Once a testing program is implemented, it must be monitored to ensure that actual practices follow these policies. Understandably, the extent to which supervisors understand the program and see its objectives as beneficial to their own are the critical variables in implementation. One area to watch is the extent to which the program is used. If no employees volunteer for the EAP or are referred to it for testing, does this mean that no substance abuse problems exist? Of course not! It simply means that supervisors are ill-informed about the program or hostile to it, or that employees are suspicious of the employer's motives!

Another area to watch is impartial application of the program. For example, if a subway driver is terminated for testing positive for cocaine and a receptionist who tested positive for marijuana is referred to an EAP, this difference in outcomes can be defended as necessary because of the difference in liability risks for the two positions. But if an "undesirable" employee is terminated for testing positive, while a "desirable" employee in the same type of position who also tests positive is given a second chance, the employer is using the substance abuse testing program illegally and immorally as a tool for selective disciplinary action.

PROBLEMS WITH TESTING, AND ALTERNATIVES TO IT

Even the strongest advocates of substance abuse testing will concede that it is an invasive and degrading procedure which is technically imperfect. And most personnel managers are concerned enough about the human resource policy issues it raises that they are implementing testing programs cautiously, if at all.[13]

And the arguments against testing are strong and compelling. A 1987 survey of 1,090 companies conducted by the American Management Association indicated that 79 percent are not testing their employees or have not developed a formal response to drug testing.[14] And of the 21 percent which are testing, only a small majority consider the effort to be effective in combating workplace substance abuse.[15]

But other research contradicts these findings, leading to the conclusion that substance abuse testing reduces absenteeism, turnover, and health care costs.[16]

The reasons for these uncertainties are not hard to elucidate. First, the drug of choice for workplace substance abusers is alcohol, which passes quickly from the body and is detectable by drug urinalysis tests for only a brief period of time. Second, drug tests determine only whether drugs are present in an employee, *not the level of concentration or the extent to which the presence of these drugs results in impaired job performance*.[17] Except for alcohol, there is no specified level of drugs in blood or urine that is accepted as an indicator of impairment. For example, the active ingredient in marijuana (THC) is stored in the fatty tissues of the body, and THC metabolites excreted in urine are detectable for thirty to sixty days following ingestion. Except for chronic users, performance effects obviously do not last that long.

Those employers who elect not to test employees as a result of these considerations should accept that some of their employees will abuse alcohol and other drugs. The question then becomes, how should these employers minimize the risks of substance abuse from the perspectives of productivity, health care costs, and risk management?

Productivity

The primary component of any program is education. Experts agree that employees who understand how and why substance abuse affects their job performance are the least likely to abuse drugs on the job.[18]

The employer should be using performance evaluation systems which appraise the performance of employees along objective performance criteria (job elements) which are known in advance to the employee and related to the primary duties of the position. If this is the case, employees who have a substance abuse problem which affects their work performance will show a record of reduced productivity, increased absenteeism, or behavioral incidents. These can be used as the basis for informal counseling and disciplinary action, just as though the underlying cause of the performance problem were something other than substance abuse.

The employer should provide health benefits which include treatment for substance abuse problems and should make information about the nature and extent of coverage available to employees during initial orientation. The information should be provided again during informal counseling if substance abuse is at all suspected as an underlying cause of the employee's performance problem. Those employees who voluntarily admit to a substance abuse problem should receive treatment. The employer should develop policies concerning disciplinary action, termination, and job retention rights for employees undergoing treatment.

Health Care Costs

The employer should continue to monitor health care costs that may indicate substance abuse problems. If health care is only available through providers at excessive costs, or if the company is too small to self-insure, it might consider leasing employees. The National Staff Leasing Association estimates that companies now lease 500,000 employees a year, up from only 150,000 in 1986. By hiring a company's workers and leasing them back, a work force leasing concern takes responsibility for the payroll and administration of benefits that smaller companies often find burdensome.[19] If the employer does provide health benefits to employees, these should also include substance abuse rehabilitation services as an essential service required of health care contractors who are selected as providers for employees within the company.

Legal Liability Risks

Legal liability risks are both increased and decreased by adopting a policy of not testing employees, and employers should be aware of the trade-offs involved. Not testing employees simply means that the employer does not have to answer any of the tough policy questions that are raised when positive test results are reported for a employee. On the other hand, this may mean that supervisors or the personnel director have no effective means of reducing the risks to clients and co-workers from a substance-abusing employee whose performance remains satisfactory and who insists that the problem either does not exist or does not affect job performance. This means waiting until a critical incident occurs—and by then it may be too late.

Public employers who wish to reduce the liability risks caused by substance abuse may wish to consider contracting for services, particularly if the contractor is bonded and responsible for civil damages of employees. In the private sector, leasing employees or the use of temporary employment agencies also achieves the same result.

SUMMARY

Employers should never test employees or applicants for substance abuse unless and until they know what they will do with the results. This means that testing is not a substance abuse control technique, but only one component of a much more comprehensive program that must be responsive to the employer's need to maintain efficiency, employees' right to privacy, and (in the case of public agencies or contractors) elected officials' right to safe and effective public services. The policy must be designed so that it is clear, well-received by employees, and legally defensible.[20]

Given its drawbacks, workplace substance abuse testing is not for every employer. But the undeniable threats to employee productivity posed by substance abuse require those employers who elect not to test applicants and employees for substance abuse to develop a range of alternative educational programs and personnel policies.

NOTES

1. A comprehensive discussion of the political, social, economic, medical, and managerial implications of substance abuse in our society is beyond the scope of this paper. They have been well documented elsewhere: Harwood, H., Napolitano, D., & Collins, J. (1984). *Economic costs to society of alcohol and drug abuse and mental illness*. Research Triangle Park, N.C.: Research Triangle Institute; Levin-Epstein, M., & Sala, S. (1986). *Alcohol and drugs in the workplace: costs, controls and controversies*. Washington, D.C.: U.S. Chamber of Commerce; Rowland, A. (1985). The cost to the U.S. economy of drug abuse. *Hearings Before the Subcommittee on Economic Goals and Intergovernmental Policy of the Joint Economic Committee*. Congress of the United States, Ninety-ninth Congress, First Session, August 6–8, MC#5522.

2. United States v. Cruikshank, 92 U.S. 542 (1875).

3. Dillon, J. (1987, May 24). How IBM uses its influence to shape drug-testing bill. *Rutland* (Vermont) *Daily Herald*, p. 1.

4. Chaves, T. (1989, January 27). Doubling in drug testing reported. (Oklahoma City) *Daily Oklahoman*, p. 1.

5. The Clearinghouse wishes to thank ASPA and its former president Robert Denhardt for supporting the drug testing survey, and SPALR and its former chair Dalmas Nelson for supporting the survey and providing initial financial support for questionnaire printing and distribution.

6. The research questions examined in this study are the following:

1. Do public agencies' personnel directors consider substance abuse a significant problem?
2. Which level of government (federal, state, or local) is most likely to consider substance abuse a significant problem?
3. Do public agencies have substance abuse policies in place? If not, are they considering adopting them?
4. Which public agencies (federal, state, or local) are most likely to have policies in place, or to be considering adopting them?
5. Do public agencies test employees and/or applicants?
6. Which public agencies (federal, state, or local) are most likely to test employees and/or applicants?
7. For which positions are public agencies most likely to test applicants?
8. When are public agencies most likely to test employees?
9. What do public agencies do with those employees or applicants who test positive?
10. What provisions are taken to ensure the protection of employee rights?
11. Are governments which have substance abuse policies in place, or are planning to adopt them, more likely to protect applicants' or employees' rights in the substance abuse testing process?
12. To what extent are Employee Assistance Programs (EAPs) used in detection or treatment of substance abuse?
13. Is there a relationship between the development of a testing policy and the utilization of EAPs by public agencies?
14. Which factors, taken together, are the best predictors of whether a public agency has a drug/alcohol policy in place, or is considering adopting one?

7. The six-page questionnaire contained four sections with closed-ended questions; answers were coded as either ordinal or interval (Likert-type scale) data:

(I) **General**: answered by all respondents ($N = 208$). Six questions on level of government, number of agency employees, perceived significance of employee substance abuse, whether or not the agency has a policy in place, or whether or not the agency is considering adopting one, and whether the agency tests applicants.

(II) **Preemployment Testing**: answered only by those respondents who report that their agencies test applicants ($N = 122$). Thirteen questions on the extent of applicant testing, which types of positions are covered, when the applicant is informed that testing will be conducted, whether written consent is required, whether refusal to submit to testing is grounds for ineligibility, whether the applicant is informed of positive test results, whether a second test is conducted to verify initial positive results, whether positive test results cause rejection of the application, whether the applicant is made aware of the fact that positive test results were the basis for refusing employment, whether positive test results are ever made available informally to other jurisdictions, whether the applicant who tested positive will ever be considered for future employment, whether conditional employment will be offered to applicants who test positive if they enroll in a treatment program, and whether this conditional employment offer is offered only to applicants for certain job classes.

(III) **Testing Current Employees**: answered only by those respondents who report that their jurisdictions test current employees ($N = 95$). Thirteen questions on the circumstances under which employees are tested, which employees are subject to testing, which job classes (if any) are subject to random testing, whether advance notice of random testing is given, whether refusal to take a test results in disciplinary action and if so which type, whether a second test is conducted to verify a positive result in the first test before disciplinary actions are taken, whether disciplinary action varies if test results are positive (depending on level of concentration, job class, or performance evaluations), what types of disciplinary action are taken if employees test positive, where employees are tested, and what type of test is used.

(IV) **Employee Assistance Programs**: answered only by those respondents who report that their agency has an employee assistance program (EAP) to provide employees with counseling and medical help with alcohol and drug abuse problems ($N = 171$). Four questions on the location of the EAP, what range of services it provides, whether it assists with evaluation and rehabilitation of employees who are substance abusers, and whether the EAP itself conducts tests.

8. The proportion of variance in the discriminant function explained by the two groups is about 43 percent (a canonical correlation of 0.4366). The Wilks's Lambda degree of separation between the two groups was 0.2391. The unstandardized canonical discriminant function coefficient (used for predicting if an agency has a policy or not) is formed by multiplying the agency's scores on each of these six variables by its coefficient, adding these partial scores to get a discriminant score, and then comparing the discriminant score to the mean average for agencies in Group 1 (those having a policy) and Group 2 (those without a policy). The Group 1 mean is -0.35274 and the Group 2 mean is 0.66138, based on the following unstandardized and standardized canonical discriminant function coefficients for each variable:

Discriminant Analysis

	Classification Function Coefficient		Canonical Discriminant Function Coefficient	
	Drug Policy	No Policy	Standardized	Unstandardized
1	1.308370	1.196931	-0.16629	-0.1098866
2	3.136055	3.364998	0.30157	0.22557551
4	2.769251	3.250845	-0.46911	0.4748871
33	15.38467	16.77325	0.48930	1.369249
36	0.8434998	0.108360	0.38682	0.2611717
37	2.111595	1.720396	-0.63132	-0.3857509
constant:	-25.42523	-28.65859		-3.03401

Therefore, knowing the responses of each agency to these six variables, it is possible to predict inclusion in Group 1 with 73.3 percent accuracy (ninety-nine out of 135 cases), and in Group 2 with 62.5 percent accuracy (forty-five out of seventy-two cases). Overall, 69.57 percent of the grouped cases can be correctly classified using discriminant analysis.

9. The questionnaire included separate questions asking whether the agency had a substance abuse testing policy in place (v3), or was considering adopting one (v5). Because several respondents ambiguously answered both questions affirmatively, the researchers analyzed each variable separately and created a dummy variable (v38) for which a positive response to either question (v3 or v5) was coded as a "yes," and a negative response to both questions was considered a "no."

10. Staudenmeier, Jr., W. (1978). Content and variation in employer policies on alcohol. *The Journal of Drug Issues, 17*(5), pp. 255–271.

11. The Clearinghouse is currently conducting additional research on the relationship to substance abuse testing of other variables such as agency structure, functions of the personnel department, and the professionalism of public personnel directors.

12. Westbrook, L. (1989, January). Why you need a crystal-clear drug policy. *Business and Health*, pp. 16–20; Turner, C. (1988, July). Drug testing: A step-by-step approach. *Business and Health*, pp. 10–14; Silverman, L. *Checklist for developing a corporate substance abuse program*. Nutley, NJ: Hoffmann-LaRoche, Inc., pp. 1–9; Pace, L., & Smits, S. (1989, May). Workplace substance abuse: Establish policies. *Personnel Journal*, p. 92; Cagney, T. (1986). *The ALMACA continuum of services: Alcohol and drug abuse in the workplace*. Arlington, VA: The Association of Labor-Management Administrators and Consultants on Alcoholism, Inc., 1986.

13. Moss, L. (1986, December). Partners for a drug-free workplace. *Across the Board*, pp. 22–30; and Miners, I., Nykodym, N., & Samerdyke-Traband, D. (1987, August). Put drug detection to the test. *Personnel*, pp. 91–97.

14. Cowan, T.R. (1987, Winter). Drugs in the workplace: To drug test or not to test. *Public Personnel Management*, p. 318.

15. Masi, D. (1987, March). Company responses to drug abuse from AMA's nationwide survey. *Personnel*, pp. 40–46.

16. McDaniel, M. (1988). Does pre-employment drug use predict on-the-job suitability? *Personnel Psychology, 41*, pp. 717–729; Evidence is skimpy that drug testing of employees works. (1989, September 7). *The Wall Street Journal*, p. B1.

17. Rosen, T.H. (1987, Fall). Identification of substance abusers in the workplace. *Public Personnel Management*, p. 200.

18. Schreier, J. (1988, October). Combating drugs at work. *Training and Development Journal, 42*(10), pp. 56–60.

19. Odds and ends. (1990, March 6). *The Wall Street Journal*, p. B1.

20. Klingner, D., O'Neill, N., and Sabet, M. (1990, Winter). Drug Testing in Public Agencies: Are Personnel Directors Doing Things Right? *Public Personnel Management, 19*(4), pp. 391–397.

5

Employee Assistance Programs

Employee assistance programs (EAPs) are a tool to help both employees and employers. They provide intake and referral services to employees whose performance levels have deteriorated due to personal problems. These problems may include, but are not restricted to, alcohol and drug abuse, emotional and family crises, and legal or financial problems.

The primary purpose of substance abuse testing is to treat and, one hopes, rehabilitate employees before their job status is irrevocably affected by substance abuse. This is why any testing program must have a treatment and rehabilitation component—the EAP.

OBJECTIVES

The purpose of this chapter is to:

1. Describe the history, objectives and functions of employee assistance programs, with particular attention to their role in the detection and treatment of substance abuse problems.

2. Assess the characteristics of an effective EAP.

3. Explore potential problems with evaluating the effectiveness of EAPs, given their conflicting objectives.

4. Show how EAPs are conceptually and operationally related to other organizational efforts (such as health promotion programs and quantity-of-work-life programs) to increase productivity, reduce health care costs, and limit liability risks.

EAPS: HISTORY, OBJECTIVES, AND FUNCTIONS

History

The forerunners of today's employee assistance programs arose during the 1930s when industrial employers began to realize that alcohol abuse and other personal problems were affecting employee safety and productivity, and that in many cases employees with personal problems could be effectively and efficiently rehabilitated.[1] This was particularly true if employers felt that personal problems were causing unintentional deviant responses by employees, and that these deviant responses could be corrected by therapeutic interventions with the employee.[2]

The number of EAPs has increased rapidly over the past few years. In 1971 there were about fifty (primarily in large private employers); today there are over ten thousand! As recently as 1985, their services were available to only a relatively small percentage of the work force (12 percent).[3] However, access has increased dramatically since then for two reasons. Private employers have increasingly felt certain that EAPs resulted in higher productivity and lower health care costs.[4] And the Federal Agency Drug Free Workplace Act (1988) and its implementing regulations required federal agencies and federal contractors to have EAPs for their employees.[5]

Objectives

The purpose of an employee assistance program (EAP) is to diagnose, treat, and rehabilitate employees whose personal problems are interfering with their work performance. From the employee's viewpoint, the objective is to treat personal problems before they have an irreparable effect on job status.[6] From the employer's viewpoint, the objective is to rehabilitate employees whose personal problems are a threat to productivity, health care costs, or legal liability, and to lay the groundwork for possible disciplinary action and discharge (if the employee cannot be rehabilitated) before these threats become a reality).[7]

Functions

Over time, both the functions of the EAP and the role of the supervisor have changed substantially and rapidly. First, while the traditional EAP was charged almost exclusively with confronting the problem of alcohol abuse, the contemporary EAP also addresses drug abuse and a range of other personal problems that may affect employee job performance. One recent survey of eighty-eight companies found that the responding firms had EAPs which provided services in the areas of alcohol, drugs, family-emotional crises, finance, legal matters, and psychiatric concerns; another showed that about 37 percent of EAP problems concern alcohol or alcohol abuse, 28 percent involve family problems, emotional problems account for 18 percent, drug abuse 8 percent, and financial or legal difficulties 5 percent.[8]

This increase in the range of functions performed by the EAP has meant that responsibility for diagnosis and treatment of personal problems is no longer a supervisory responsibility, if indeed it ever was. Today the supervisor is expected to observe and record changes in employees' behavior and job performance. The documentation can be used to discipline employees and to refer them to the EAP for professional diagnosis and treatment.

And while EAPs' proponents may take heart from statistics chronicling the growth in the number of EAPs or the range of functions they perform, other observers might reasonably wonder whether focusing attention on whether or not employees are covered by an EAP only serves to deflect attention from more critical assessments of the EAP's characteristics and performance. But focusing attention on the number of EAPs or the number of employees covered by them, researchers tend to ignore more critical substantive issues: Have employers endorsed the concept of the EAP for its value in rehabilitation and productivity or as a sort of legal insurance policy against employee grievances and lawsuits arising out of disciplinary action?[9]

CHARACTERISTICS OF AN EFFECTIVE EAP

There is no typical EAP. Rather, the nature and composition of EAPs vary from organization to organization. One of the principles upon which they are based is that each organization is unique and each organization's EAP should reflect this uniqueness.[10]

But this variability notwithstanding, all effective EAPs do perform four essential functions: client referral and needs assessment, provision of services, program integration and administration, and program evaluation.

Client Referral and Needs Assessment

An EAP assesses the needs of individual employees who present themselves to it. Employees may refer themselves or be referred by someone else such as a friend, relative, co-worker, or supervisor. This results in a medical treatment model (one which follows medical procedures and values), even if the services provided are nonmedical (such as financial counseling). That is, records are kept within the EAP only and are not disclosed to any outside source except upon the written authorization of the employee.

Referral and treatment methods should be appropriate to the demographics of the population as well as the nature of the problem.[11]

Provision of Services

There are legitimate differences of opinion as to whether the EAP should focus on abuse of alcohol and other substances or on a much broader agenda. Whatever range of objectives is selected, the EAP should provide comprehensive high-quality clinical services, supervisory training, management consultation, and preventive health education/health promotion services appropriate to the needs of the employer. The services must competently evaluate employees and appropriately assist them in returning to and/or remaining effective in their jobs when alcohol, drug abuse, mental health problems, or other events alter their work performance capacity. The EAP must have an established community referral network and coordinate its services with local resources, health organizations, and self-help groups as appropriate.

While inpatient treatment is at times a necessary first step for substance abusers, a well-structured and medically supervised outpatient program is frequently just as effective. And it can do the job at a third the cost, while keeping the employee on the job.[12]

Program Integration and Administration

There are two structural alternatives for operating an EAP: internal and external.

In the external EAP, an employee needing assistance of one kind or another is referred outside the organization to a community-based or privately run service. In the internally run service, employees can receive assistance through resources available inside the firm. In between are the variations on these two basic forms where employees obtain some services internally, some externally, and in some cases have a choice between in-house or outside services.[13]

For an internal EAP to be cost effective, the employer should have at least 2,000 employees.[14] This makes it an unattractive alternative for most employers, though it does have the advantages of ready accessibility by employees and ready availability if crisis intervention services are required. But it raises more issues of confidentiality and liability than does the external option.[15]

If an internal EAP is selected as the appropriate option, it should be designed to assure its integration into the structures and processes guiding the overall administration and management of the company or agency. The EAP should be run by a director with access to and involvement with top management of the agency, with sufficient resources and qualified staff to make a measurable impact on the problem. The EAP director should be assisted by an advisory board including supervisors, employees, and union officials to ensure its responsiveness to employee and employer needs.[16]

There are several types of external EAPs which may fit the employer's needs. The employer may assess employees internally and contract with several outside agencies to provide specific referral services, contract with one EAP that assesses employees' needs and refers them to appropriate community resources or subcontractors, or contract with one outside consultant to provide the full range of EAP services.[17]

With the increasing demand for EAP services and the advantages of contracting out for them, it is not surprising that there are thousands of EAP providers around the United States today. This means human resource management professionals should be prepared to develop and enforce contract provisions which will provide desired services at a predictable and reasonable cost.[18]

Concrete criteria for EAP effectiveness are hard to come by. But one expert states that the EAP

> should see and refer for drug-abuse treatment at least 1% of the work force each year. To do this, the program must be properly staffed. Generally this means one full-time equivalent assessment and referral professional for every 3,500 to 4,200 employees, plus adequate clerical support.[19]

Unfortunately, however, a number of studies indicate that while there are few significant differences between public- and private-sector EAPs, they both tend to be underdeveloped and poorly integrated into a company or agency.[20] In response, a number of agencies and interest groups have begun to develop standards for evaluating EAP performance.[21] And the mental health care industry is increasingly regulated by outside professional reviews of the appropriateness and efficiency of EAP services.[22]

The EAP should have policies and procedures in effect aimed at assuring the appropriateness, effectiveness, and efficiency of the program in meeting the needs of both management and the employee population served. The procedures must be consistent with applicable law and employer policies and procedures. This includes availability of a sufficient number of qualified counselors, services provided in an appropriate office space that assures easy access and privacy, a case record system in compliance with confidentiality laws and policies, guidelines for measuring or assessing the quality of care, and regular review of program services.

An EAP should have a mechanism in place to evaluate the appropriateness, effectiveness, and efficiency of the delivery of services and program integration. Evaluations of the appropriateness of client services, educational programs, supervisory training, and outreach activities should be performed on an annual basis and become a part of the permanent program records. Descriptive statistics should be employed whenever possible to summarize program activities and facilitate the annual evaluation. Program modifications should be made on the basis of evaluations.

EAP EVALUATION CRITERIA

Today, the employee assistance program has become almost a mandatory element of the employer's response to substance abuse. And this makes sense. Employers understand that substance abuse has been demonstrated to reduce productivity, increase health care costs, and increase liability risks, so they are generally willing to support programs that promise to treat the problem. And EAP providers invariably play into this presumption by claiming that the EAP will "save time and money, help managers manage better, add value to your employee benefits package, and improve morale and productivity."[23] It would be nice if all of these claims were valid. However, claims of "cures" in the substance abuse treatment field must be viewed with skepticism, since the success rate is always less than half and often as low as 5 percent or 10 percent. The majority relapse within a year after undergoing treatment.[24] So experts caution that valid (independently verifiable) program effectiveness and cost effectiveness data are hard to come by from EAP vendors. Starr and Byram point out that

> Potential contracting organizations could be asked to provide data on referral rates, insurance utilization, turnover and absenteeism rates; however, there may be a shortage of this type of information, and appraisals may be bolstered speculatively by estimates that are based on data from other contexts, regions or target populations.[25]

And Hellan and Campbell point out that

> In addition to those cost considerations that are brought to the purchase of any new product or service, the personnel administrator should ask about the fee structure. How is it determined? What sort of increases can be expected after the first year or two? Companies sometimes incur greater EAP costs than originally anticipated precisely because these questions weren't asked.[26]

A more fundamental problem with evaluation of external EAPs is that their primary advantage (confidentiality) frequently makes it difficult to collect the "hard" data needed to prove their effectiveness. Although many EAPs appear to be worthwhile, it is often difficult if not impossible to determine the extent to which changes in employee behavior are due to the EAP. Yet it is absolutely necessary that these data be available if the EAP is to achieve clear goals efficiently.[27]

EAP, HPP, AND QWL

EAPs have developed rapidly in the past few years because their presence is mandated by the provisions of the Drug Free Workplace Act for federal agencies and contractors. And they have a historical record in the private sector of effectively using constructive confrontation and counseling for dealing with workplace substance abusers. The American Management Association reported that more than half (51 percent) of major firms supported EAPS for drug abusers in 1988, up from 42 percent the year before.[28]

In many organizations, practitioners have begun to augment the EAP approach to substance abuse by combining it with two alternative approaches which recognize the close relationship between substance abuse and workplace conditions: health promotion programs (HPPs) and quality of work life (QWL) efforts.[29]

It is necessary to relate the employee assistance program to the larger organizational context and structure because a review of relevant literature identifies four perspectives adopted by social scientists studying drinking behavior and the workplace.[30] The work culture perspective postulates that administrative and occupational subcultures establish norms for alcohol use. The social control perspective postulates that an organization's disciplinary structure may either inhibit or create opportunities for the development of drinking problems. The alienation perspective and the work stress perspective postulate that various workplace conditions (such as boring tasks or work overload) cause distress, which employees may seek to relieve with alcohol.[31]

The EAP is sometimes effective at treating substance abuse problems in the individual employees; cooperation with HPP and QWL practitioners is necessary to address workplace factors related to substance abuse problems.[32] But it is frequently difficult to clearly document (using empirical data derived from controlled longitudinal studies) the impact of HPP or QWL interventions on employee productivity. And in turn, the relationship of EAPs to HPP and QWL programs means that EAP advocates must address the same dilemmas of underlying objectives that have dogged these other programs in recent years. For example, does the EAP have a legitimate role in the medicalization of employee personality issues that affect performance, or are these protected by the employee's right to privacy? And is the primary purpose of the EAP to meet the emotional needs of the employee, the productivity concerns of the manager, or the risk-management needs of the company or agency attorney?[33]

SUMMARY

Employee assistance programs are a traditional organizational technique for treating alcoholism. Today, there is an increasing tendency to expand their role to include not only other forms of substance abuse but also other personal problems which impact on employee productivity.[34] The effectiveness of EAPs at treating alcoholism is heavily documented by economic data. Private employers presume that they will be equally effective at increasing productivity by combatting drug abuse; and public employers create them because they are mandated by law for federal agencies and federal contractors, or they consider them a form of legal insurance against lawsuits resulting from the employer's efforts to discipline substance abusers.[35] While some commentators consider EAPs to be most effective when they focus on clearly defined substance abuse problems rather than general emotional treatment needs or public health issues,[36] others favor a more broadly defined intervention and treatment role.

NOTES

1. Steele, P. (1988). Substance abuse and the work place, with special attention to employee assistance programs: An overview. *The Journal of Applied Behavioral Science, 24*(4), pp. 315–325; and McClellan, K. (1985, August). The changing nature of EAP practice. *Personnel Administrator, 30*(8), pp. 29–37.

2. Sonnenstuhl, W. (1986). *Inside an emotional health program: A field study of workplace assistance for troubled employees*. Ithaca, NY: Industrial Labor Relations Press.

3. Reidiger, A. (1985). EAPs: barriers to effectiveness. In Klarreich, S., Francek, J., & Moore, C. (Eds.). *The human resources management handbook: Principles and practice of employee assistance programs*. New York: Praeger, pp. 393–408.

4. McDonnell Douglas Corporation employee assistance program financial offset study, 1985–1988. (1989). Westport, CT: Alexander & Alexander Consulting Group; Starr, A., & Byram, G. (1985, August). Cost/benefit analysis for employee assistance programs. *Personnel Administrator, 30*(8), pp. 55–60.

5. U.S. Department of Health and Human Services. (1986, December). *Standards and criteria for the development and evaluation of a comprehensive employee assistance program*. Washington, D.C.: Public Health Service, Health Resources and Services Administration, Bureau of Health Care Delivery and Assistance, Division of Federal Occupational and Beneficiary Health Services.

6. Sloan, R., & Gruman, J. (1988, Fall). Participation in workplace health promotion programs: The contribution of health and organizational factors. *Health Education Quarterly, 15*(3), pp. 269–288.

7. Bowers, M., DeCenzo, D., Walton, C., & Grazer, W. (1989, October). What do employers see as the benefits of assistance programs? *Risk Management, 36*(10), pp. 46–50.

8. Brumback, C. (1987, April-June). EAPs: Bringing health and productivity to the workplace. *Business, 37*, pp. 42–45.

9. Starr, A., & Byram, G. (1985, August). Cost/benefit analysis for employee assistance programs. *Personnel Administrator, 30*(8), pp. 55–60.

10. Hollmann, R. (1981, September). Beyond contemporary employee assistance programs. *Personnel Administrator, 26*(9), pp. 37–41.

11. Johnson, A. (1985, May-June). Municipal employee assistance programs. *Public Administration Review, 45*(3), pp. 383–390; and Boyce, J. (1990, April 10). Tailoring treatment for black addicts. *The Wall Street Journal*, pp. B1, 2.

12. Frabotta, J. (1989, February). How to weigh drug treatment options. *Business and Health*, pp. 37–38.

13. Ford, R., & McLaughlin, F. (1981, September). Employee assistance programs: A descriptive survey of ASPA members. *Personnel Administrator, 26*(9), pp. 29–35.

14. Wakefield, M. (1984, June 26). *The basics of EAPs*. (audio tape). Employee assistance programs workshop, The Mental Health Association of Dade County, Miami, FL.

15. Jones, O. (1985). The rationale and critical issues of EAP development. In Klarreich, S., Francek, J., & Moore, C. (Eds.). *The human resources management handbook: Prin-*

ciples and practice of employee assistance programs. New York: Praeger, pp. 7–12; and Lyons, P. (1987). EAPs, the only real cure for substance abuse. *Management Review, 76*(3), pp. 39–41.

16. Brumback, C. (1987, April-June). EAPs: bringing health and productivity to the workplace. *Business, 37*, pp. 42–45.

17. Hellan, R. (1986, June). Employee assistance, an EAP update: A perspective for the '80s. *Personnel Journal, 26*(9), pp. 51–54; and Isenberg, S. (1985). EAP service center model. In Klarreich, S., Francek, J., & Moore, C. (Eds.). *The human resources management handbook: Principles and practice of employee assistance programs.* New York: Praeger, pp. 58–68.

18. Chiabotta, B. (1985, August). Evaluating the EAP vendors. *Personnel Administrator, 30*(8), pp. 39–43; and Hellan, R., & Campbell, W. (1986, June). Contracting for EAP services. *Personnel Administrator, 26*(9), pp. 46–51.

19. Wrich, J. (1988, January-February). Beyond testing: Coping with drugs at work. *Harvard Business Review*, p. 124.

20. Johnson, A. (1986, Spring). A comparison of employee assistance programs in corporate and government organizational contexts. *Review of Public Personnel Administration, 6*(2), pp. 28–42.

21. U.S. Department of Health and Human Services. (1987). *Standards for employee alcoholism and/or assistance programs.* Washington, D.C.: Public Health Service, Alcohol, Drug Abuse, and Mental Health Administration, National Institute on Drug Abuse; and U.S. Department of Health and Human Services. (1986, December). *Standards and criteria for the development of a comprehensive employee assistance program.* Washington, D.C.: Public Health Service, Health Resources and Services Administration, Bureau of Health Care Delivery and Assistance, Division of Federal Occupational and Beneficiary Health Services.

22. Batten, R., & Mellor, N. (1986, Spring). The agency review system. *Journal of Drug Issues*, pp. 295–301.

23. Sales brochure from Personal Performance Consultants, Inc. (an EAP provider), and cover letter from Deborah Sheperis, National Sales Director, April 4, 1988.

24. Bacon, K. (1989, September 6). Effective treatments: Little is known. *The Wall Street Journal*, p. A11; Weiss, R. (1987). Writing under the influence: Science versus fiction in the analysis of corporate alcoholism programs. *Personnel Psychology, 40*, pp. 341–355; Schuckit, M. (1988, May). Prediction of outcome among alcoholics. *Drug Abuse & Alcoholism Newsletter, 17*(4), pp. 1–4; and Donkin, R. (1989, October). The revolving door of addiction. *Business and Health*, pp. 16–20.

25. Starr, A., & Byram, G. (1985, August). Cost/benefit analysis for employee assistance programs. *Personnel Administrator, 30*(8), pp. 55–60.

26. Hellan, R., & Campbell, W. (1986, June). Contracting for EAP services. *Personnel Administrator, 26*(9), p. 51.

27. Donkin, R. (1989, February). The new mental health watchdogs: Can they deliver? *Business and Health*, pp. 16–18; William Mercer-Neidinger-Hansen, Inc. (1989, January 30). Substance abuse in the workforce: A survey of employees. *Medical Benefits, 6*(2), p. 7; and Durking, W. (1985). Evaluation of EAP programming. In Klarreich, S., Francek, J., & Moore, C. (Eds.) *The human resources management handbook: Principles and practice of employee assistance programs.* New York: Praeger, 1985, pp. 243–259.

28. Companies do more than test for drugs. (1990, June 1). *The Wall Street Journal*, p. B1.

29. Roman, P., & Blum, T. (1988). Formal intervention in employee health: Comparisons of the nature and structure of employee assistance programs and health promotion programs. *Social Science Medicine*, 26(5), pp. 503–514; Steele, P. (1988). Substance abuse and the work place, with special attention to employee assistance programs: An overview. *The Journal of Applied Behavioral Science*, 24(4), pp. 315–325; and Shain, M., Survali, J., & Boutilier, M. (1986). *Healthier workers: Health promotion and employee assistance programs*. Lexington, MA: Lexington Books.

30. Sonnenstuhl, W., & Trice, H. (1988). Drinking behavior and risk factors related to the work place: Implications for research and prevention. *The Journal of Applied Behavioral Science*, 24(4), pp. 327–346.

31. Rundle, R. (1990, February 15). U-Haul puts high price on vices of its workers. *The Wall Street Journal*, pp. B1, 10.

32. Sonnenstuhl, W. (1988, November). Contrasting employee assistance, health promotion, and quality of work life programs and their effects on alcohol abuse and dependence. *Journal of Applied Behavioral Science*, 24, pp. 347–363; and Sonnenstuhl, W., & Trice, H. (1988). Drinking behavior and risk factors related to the work place: Implications for research and prevention. *The Journal of Applied Behavioral Science*, 24(4), pp. 327–346.

33. Sonnenstuhl, W. (1986). *Inside an emotional health program: A field study of workplace assistance for troubled employees*. Ithaca, NY: ILR Press, New York State School of Industrial and Labor Relations, Cornell University.

34. Trice, H., & Sonnenstuhl, W. (1989, Summer). Perspectives on job-based programs for alcohol and drug problems II: Introduction. *Journal of Drug Issues*, pp. 315–316.

35. Scanlon, W. (1986). *Alcoholism and drug abuse in the workplace: Employee assistance programs*. New York: Praeger.

36. Sonnenstuhl, W., & Trice, H. (1986). *Strategies for employee assistance programs: The crucial balance (key issues—number 30)*. Ithaca, NY: ILR Press, New York State School of Industrial and Labor Relations, Cornell University.

6

Working with
Employees and Unions

Most major public- and private-sector employers have by now made a decision to routinely test applicants for substance abuse. Or they will soon make this decision. Michael Walsh, head of behavioral and clinical pharmacology at the National Institute on Drug Abuse, predicts that substance abuse testing will be a standard requirement to get a job with a public agency or major private sector employer within five years.[1] By this time, employers will have decided that the risks of substance abuse outweigh the indignities and uncertainties of testing or interpreting test results.[2]

Let's assume that an employer has decided to routinely test applicants for substance abuse and to test employees under specified circumstances. Top managers are convinced that the potential costs and risks of substance abuse testing are outweighed by the need to maintain productivity, keep a cap on health care costs, or reduce liability risks.

But even the strongest advocates of substance abuse testing will concede that it is an invasive and degrading procedure which is vulnerable to technical and human error.[3] And most personnel managers are concerned about the human resource pol-

icy issues it raises. This means that once the employer has decided to test employees for substance abuse and has addressed the policy issues raised in Chapter 4,
critical human relations issues need to be addressed if the employer is to "sell"
substance abuse testing to employees. And unless these issues are addressed, substance abuse testing is likely to be less successful because of employee antipathy
or resistance.

OBJECTIVES

The purpose of this chapter is to:

1. Tell management how employees feel about substance abuse.
2. Enable management to understand better how employees feel about
   substance abuse testing.
3. Train supervisors to manage for productivity, detect signs of deteriorating job performance, document, and constructively counsel unproductive employees.
4. If the employer is operating under a collective bargaining agreement
   with a union or employee association, explore some ways of constructively involving the union in the development and revision of testing
   policies and procedures.
5. Present the results of a case study that confirms these conclusions with
   empirical evidence.

HOW DO EMPLOYEES FEEL ABOUT SUBSTANCE ABUSE?

While objective sources agree that substance abuse is a problem in the workplace, employees are less certain. Nor is there any agreement among employees as
to the causes of substance abuse or its relationship (if any) to workplace conditions.
The results from a national sample of young adults suggest little concentration of
drug users or on-the-job drug use in specific occupations or industries.[4] This confirms the findings of previous studies reporting no differences in alcohol prevalence
across broad occupational or industrial classes.[5] However, some other research suggests that the employees most likely to work under the influence of alcohol or other
drugs are men younger than thirty, and that the likelihood of employees doing so
increases when they feel unhappy about their jobs and socialize frequently with co-
workers off the job.[6]

Given these results, it is clear that we must continue to look toward societal values and conditions as the key to workplace substance abuse.[7] Under these conditions, it makes sense that employees are quite tolerant of light drinking among their
colleagues and reasonably tolerant of occasional recreational drug use.[8] This means
that employees are sophisticated about the real dangers of substance abuse, but they

also tend to discount much of the anti-drug propaganda that has come out of the war on drugs. For example, one recent study reports that neither chronic nor current use of marijuana or alcohol had adversely affected the subjects' occupational status and achievement in middle adulthood.[9] This means that our propensity to treat workplace alcohol abuse as an individual problem may not be successful, though it may also be the most promising approach to take.

Ironically, the war on drugs that has made many recreational drugs illegal has also removed some of the social pressures against their use. Today it is commonplace for tobacco smokers and heavy drinkers to feel defensive about their drug habits because their friends and colleagues feel free to criticize them. This means that co-workers are a valuable source of valid information about the risks of drug use. But because illegal drug users tend to hide their habits or to indulge only around fellow users, this element of social control is absent.[10]

Employees are also justified in discounting anti-drug propaganda because substance abuse is just one of many causes of poor employee job performance. Initially, faulty personnel systems or practices may result in the hiring of unqualified employees, inadequate orientation to job expectations, inadequate feedback, and inadequate consequences for desirable or undesirable performance.[11] In addition, emotional disorders cost employers billions in lost productivity, and cause just as many problems in interpersonal relationships as do substance abuse.[12] And while irritability and hangovers from substance abuse are temporary, emotional problems are often permanent.

HOW DO EMPLOYEES FEEL ABOUT SUBSTANCE ABUSE TESTING?

Although there is general recognition that employee attitudes toward substance abuse and substance abuse testing are an important variable to be considered in implementing drug testing program, little research has been conducted concerning this topic.[13] However, the more employers know about employee attitudes, the more likely they are to develop policies and implement programs that employees consider fair and beneficial to both the employer and the employee.

The bottom line is: They don't like it! Unfortunately for managers, there is little correlation between employee substance abuse and negative attitudes toward substance abuse testing. If that were the case, we wouldn't have to test at all—just ask employees how they felt about testing, and test only those who oppose it!

In reality, the issue is much more complex. How employees feel about substance abuse testing can be affected by a number of factors: what they perceive to be the purpose of the program, whether they feel the implementation of the program is justified by the extent of the problem, whether they feel the sample collection process is handled in such a way as to minimize its invasive and dehumanizing aspects, and whether the primary objective of the program for those who test positive is rehabilitation—regardless of the substance involved, whether the program is implemented fairly, and whether employee rights to privacy and job security are scrupulously protected. Ironically, a substance abuse testing program can itself contribute to the feelings of powerlessness and self-estrangement which worsen employees' substance abuse problems.[14]

Employees will object to any program that tests employees in lower-status occupations while declining to test employees in higher-status occupations (even though these employees may perform the same type of work and run the same liability risks). For example, the American Civil Liberties Union (ACLU) filed suit recently on behalf of nurses at a hospital when doctors on the hospital staff were excluded from substance abuse testing requirements.[15]

HOW CAN MANAGEMENT HELP EMPLOYEES DEVELOP POSITIVE ATTITUDES TOWARD SUBSTANCE ABUSE TESTING PROGRAMS?

The key here is you don't try to help employees develop positive attitudes toward testing itself. This is an unreasonable expectation. Instead, you give them a clear understanding of why substance abuse is a workplace problem and how testing is necessary to detect and combat it. Then you show how the primary purpose of the program is education, treatment, and rehabilitation of substance-abusing employees. There is considerable research support for the idea that employees support employee assistance programs and are more willing to participate in them if their reactions to these programs are positive and based on concrete information.[16]

Another key is by emphasizing the stake all employees have in productivity improvement (not covering for someone else or doing their work), the stake all employees have in reducing health care costs (not paying higher premiums for the sake of someone else with a riskier lifestyle), and the stake all employees have in reducing liability risks (particularly if the company is employee-owned and/or self-insured).[17]

Nor should substance abuse policies and programs be directed solely toward employees. Managers and professional employees are also likely to be substance abusers because of the nature of their work and the high stress levels connected with it.

TRAINING SUPERVISORS

The key to selling the program to supervisors is to not let management deflect the purpose of the program away from productivity improvement, reduced health care costs, or reduced liability risks. These are all objectives most supervisors (and employees) can identify with.

Any effort by management to use the program as a means of disciplinary action without prior attempts at rehabilitation should be avoided (regardless of whether the employee with the substance abuse problem is "good" or "bad"). Any attempt by management to implement the program in ways which counter its expressed objectives should be resisted, as should any attempts by unauthorized persons inside or outside the organization to obtain the identities of employees who have been referred to the EAP for a substance abuse problem, the nature of the problem, or its disposition.

This means that supervisors need to be carefully and thoroughly trained to recognize performance problems and to respond appropriately. Employees must be oriented with this same information so that they will be informed as to how the program works in practice and comfortable with its procedures.

Managing for Productivity

The supervisor must be sure that management has met its responsibilities. That is,

- Do employees have adequate skills or training to perform the duties expected of them?
- Are the performance expectations clear?
- Are employees provided with adequate feedback from management (the supervisor) concerning their performance?
- Does good or bad performance invoke equitable consequences which are meaningful to the employee and clearly related to employee performance?[18]

Detecting Deteriorating Job Performance

Normally, a pattern of declining job performance occurs over a period of weeks or months. This makes it important that the supervisor observe and document specific incidents that indicate deteriorating job performance.

1. *Absence or tardiness:*
   - taking excessive time off sick
   - repeated, unscheduled absences or tardiness on Mondays or Fridays, before and after holidays, or after paydays
   - leaving work early for a variety of reasons
   - taking longer lunch breaks or coffee breaks
   - leaving the work area more than necessary.

2. *Quality and quantity of work:*
   - alternating periods of high and low work productivity
   - making excessive mistakes
   - making poor judgments or decisions
   - missing deadlines

- wasting materials used on the job
- slow at starting and completing assigned tasks.

3. *Attitude and mood:*
   - periods of high, then low, morale
   - overreacting to criticism
   - avoiding talking with supervisor regarding work issues
   - difficulty in remembering directions or details
   - difficulty in dealing with complex tasks
   - work requires more time and effort than usual
   - mood changes after lunch or break.

4. *Relationships with fellow employees:*
   - complaints from co-workers about the employee
   - more intolerant; resentful of fellow employees
   - complaints from outside sources (customers, clients, other companies or agencies).

5. *Physical appearance:*
   - deterioration of personal appearance or personal hygiene
   - increased nervousness and shakiness
   - changes in appearance after lunch or break.

6. *Accidents:*
   - an increase in accidents on and off the job that interfere with job performance.

Documentation

The purpose of documentation is to provide a contemporaneous written record of these objective performance incidents which can be used in an interview with the employee and for subsequent referral to the EAP. With documentation, the opportunity for a positive interview and an objective referral to the EAP is created. Without it, there is a high probability that the employee will offer conflicting versions of reality and deny the performance deficiencies. This means that the interview will not be productive, and the chance of the employee contacting the EAP voluntarily is diminished.

Documentation should include all of the significant elements, including

- date, time and location of incidents
- names of witnesses
- performance or behavior exhibited by the employee
- consequences of that action or behavior on the employee's total work performance, and/or the operations of the work unit
- the response of the supervisor to the employee's action or behavior.

The availability of these records will enable supervisors to refer to specific behaviors and events when dealing with an employee. These records are essential if disciplinary action taken against the employee is appealed, in that documentation is the basis for justifying the employer's actions to an arbitrator. When preparing documentation, it may be helpful to review the following checklist to ensure completeness and accuracy:

- Record while your memory is still fresh
- Indicate the date, time, and location of the incident(s)
- Record the employee's actions or the behavior exhibited
- Indicate the person(s) or work product(s) involved
- List the specific performance standard(s) violated or exceeded
- Record the consequences of the action or behavior (oral or written reprimand, suspension, etc.)
- List the deadlines for completion of work still pending, timeframes for changing behavior, and the consequences (including disciplinary action) for continued deficient performance
- Be objective—record observations, not impressions
- Indicate the employee's reaction to efforts to modify his or her behavior.

Counseling the Employee Constructively

Supervisors routinely discuss an employee's performance with the employee. But if the normal processes of training, delegation, and feedback are ineffective at improving the employee's performance, the supervisor must reluctantly contemplate the reality that performance will not improve without counseling the employee. A constructive counseling interview is designed to avoid confrontation, not encourage it! It is supposed to lead to performance improvement by making the rational employee aware that he/she is responsible for the consequences of his/her deficient performance, or to contact the employee assistance program if the performance deficiency is caused by a personal problem such as substance abuse. The following guidelines are recommended.

1. *In advance of the interview:*
Make an appointment with the employee to discuss job performance. Set a specific time and place for the interview to occur. May sure the interview will be completely private, without any interruptions from visitors or phone calls. Allow sufficient time. Make sure documentation is available. Be prepared to show the employee specific, documented incidents so that the record speaks for itself.

2. *During the interview:*
Make sure your manner combines firmness and consideration, so that the employee understands both that the performance problem is serious and that you are

seriously interested in helping him or her. Thank the employee for coming. Do not smoke if this bothers the employee. Consider whether your desk is a barrier to communication.

Remember that consistent and clear communication is necessary for job performance to improve. Occasional warnings or ignoring the problem will just make it worse and are an abdication of supervisory responsibility for both employee productivity and employee welfare. Once the interview has started, *don't* be afraid to get involved. You already are. Focus the interview on job performance deficiencies, while acknowledging your employee's positive contributions. Have on hand documentation of declining job performance or violations of personnel rules. Avoid cross-examining the employee or otherwise giving the impression that you intend to pry into the employee's private life. By continuing to emphasize that the employee is responsible for job-related performance deficiencies and their consequences, you keep the employee from "turning the tables" and criticizing your own performance or that of other employees. You also keep employees from reacting so defensively if they feel they themselves or their right to privacy are under attack.

Work toward making an agreement with the employee that he or she is responsible for improving performance deficiencies. Do not show any anger or frustration, regardless of how you feel. Do not threaten the employee, but be clear about the consequences of continued substandard performance. Tell the employee that you will continue to monitor and document job performance, and that disciplinary action will be necessary if there is no significant performance improvement.

If it appears that personal problems are responsible for the performance deficiency, urge the employee to contact the employee assistance program voluntarily. If the union steward is present, encourage his or her support of the help being offered.

After the Interview

Document the counseling interview by having the employee sign a confirmation of the goals and the timeframe for improvement and any steps you have jointly agreed to. Continue to document the employee's performance. Encourage and support the employee in the event that performance improves, whether this improvement is sudden or gradual.

After Referral to the Employee Assistance Program

If the employee voluntarily contacts the employee assistance program, it is most probable that you will not even know it. In this case, the only result of the counseling interview that you will be able to observe is the employee's subsequent performance.

If the employee is referred to the employee assistance program involuntarily, work with the EAP counselor so that the referral will be effective from both the employer's and the employee's points of view. Provide the EAP counselor with documentation of the employee's performance problem and brief this person with the content and outcome of the counseling interview which resulted in the referral of the employee to the EAP.

When the employee is rehabilitated and returns to work, continue to observe and monitor work performance as before. If the employee fails to perform up to previously established performance standards, the supervisor must follow through on established disciplinary procedures. If the employee does perform up to these standards, the supervisor can justifiably take satisfaction in the fact that his or her concern and intervention both avoided the need for formal discipline and helped remedy a personal problem that threatened the employee's job security.

IF YOU BARGAIN COLLECTIVELY

Collective bargaining complicates the process of implementing a substance abuse testing program because it indroduces a third party—the union or employee association—into what had previously been a two-party relationship (employer-employee). It does not necessarily make the implementation process more difficult, because the union can be a powerful ally if it is treated with respect and encouraged to participate in the development and implementation of substance abuse testing policies and programs. It does mean than management should recognize that the union's initial reaction to management's proposing a substance abuse testing program will be suspicion, if not outright hostility.[19]

Here's how to implement substance abuse testing without incurring this reaction. First, the employer should recognize that increasing awareness of workplace substance abuse places the union in a difficult position. On the one hand, unions recognize that the problems caused by employee substance abuse (low productivity, increased health care costs, and increased liability risks) are legitimate concerns of both labor and management. On the other hand, the union is obligated to protect its members' rights against unfair, unreasonable, and possibly unconstitutional testing procedures. Just as it is unfair for the union to criticize all management attempts to control substance abuse as unwarranted, so it is unfair for management to criticize the union as being inherently and unalterably opposed to all substance abuse programs implemented by management.

With this in mind, the employer should recognize that the first essential step is to cooperate fully with the union by involving them completely in the development and implementation of any substance abuse program that is being contemplated. This includes the collection or analysis of data on the extent of the problem, the development of proposals to combat it, the negotiation of those proposals as part of a collective bargaining agreement, and the effective and fair administration of the program once it has become company (or agency) policy.

Initially, the company or agency may wish to start by implementing some of the steps to combat workplace substance abuse without implementing a testing program. This can include increased monitoring of employee productivity, increased education and training for employees of the personal and organizational problems caused by substance abuse, making available employee assistance programs or EAP services outside the employer on a voluntary basis, and the institution of progressive discipline following informal counseling for performance deficiencies, even if substance abuse is suspected as the underlying cause of the performance problem. All of these programs can be instituted easily and unilaterally by management, provided the union is involved at the outset, because their intent is not only to increase productivity but to help employees (on a voluntary basis) with personal problems that are beginning to affect productivity. Even the most adversarial union will support these measures, unless past managerial practices give them cause to suspect the employer's intentions.

The employer may also be able to unilaterally initiate mandatory testing of applicants. These people are not union members at the time of application, nor is the union normally interested in protecting their rights until they have been hired, become dues-paying members, and have passed their probationary period. Even if the union suspects that the employer intends eventually to implement substance abuse testing for employees as well, applicant testing is still a legitimate means of gaining information about applicants, learning more about the testing process and employee reactions to it, and reducing the risks of workplace substance abuse for new employees.

If the employer does decide to implement substance abuse testing of current employees, this should never be done unilaterally.[20] At the very least, it will antagonize the union unnecessarily, in that union leaders will be forced by their members to react strongly against testing if it is presented as a nonnegotiable change in working conditions. The union will file a grievance against testing or allege that the unilateral imposition of a substance abuse testing for employees is an unfair labor practice. The collective bargaining regulatory agency (such as the National Labor Relations Board in the private sector) or the courts will order bargaining with respect to this issue, and management will be required to negotiate anyway. It would have been simpler and more constructive to have discussed the proposal with the union in the first place, either informally or formally during contract negotiations.

An employer who wishes to implement substance abuse testing for employees should carefully develop a complete policy covering the critical policy issues discussed in Chapter 4. Particular attention should be given to those aspects of the testing policy or procedure which are most likely to be resisted by the union as violative of employee rights and to those aspects which are potentially most capable of winning union support through their emphasis on rehabilitation and protection of employee rights. Here are some particularly critical areas:

The basis for testing must be clearly established. Unions will generally object to all random or universal testing as a violation of employees' individual rights. An employer who wishes to implement such testing must be prepared to face a court challenge or be supported by previous court decisions establishing the legitimacy of such testing on the basis of the need for public health and safety or the "sensitive" nature of the position. Also, an employer who wishes to test employees on the basis of "reasonable suspicion" must be prepared to define this operationally, and have demonstrated that supervisors (or whoever makes this determination) have the skills to knowledgeably and fairly refer employees for testing.

The employer must solicit the union's help to ensure that the testing procedure itself (collection, handling, analysis, and storage of the sample) will be done according to appropriate technical standards so that the possibility of false positives is reduced to a minimum. The invasiveness and indignities of the collection process itself must be minimized insofar as possible.

Management should solicit and follow union suggestions designed to protect the confidentiality of the testing process and the referral of employees who test positive to the employee assistance program.

Management should join with the union in affirming that substance abuse (whether of alcohol, prescription drugs, or illegal drugs) is an illness. The employer should affirm that the primary objective of substance abuse testing is to provide helpful treatment to employees before their personal problems (including substance abuse) have an irreparable effect on their job performance or employment status.

Management should pledge to continually involve the union in the development, implementation, and evaluation of the substance abuse testing program—not only of testing itself, but of the effectiveness of the EAP. The objective of the EAP itself should be rehabilitation. The EAP should be supported, staffed, operated, and evaluated in such a manner as to ensure that it can realistically be expected to meet its objectives. The characteristics of the EAP, the services it provides, and the relative contributions of employees and the employer to the cost of those services are all legitimate items for inclusion within the scope of a collective bargaining agreement.

Once a union has agreed to accept employee substance abuse testing, it will be concerned about specific contract language implementing the elements of a testing policy. Management may wish to accept the inclusion of contract provisions such as the following in order to cement union support for the program.[21]

1. *General Testing Policy*

- The employer will bargain with the union before implementing any aspect or change in substance abuse testing policy.
- All employees will be clearly informed of what drugs or substances are prohibited.
- The employer will provide an educational program aimed at heightening the awareness of drug- and alcohol-related problems and treatment alternatives.
- The testing policy shall not pertain to any substances consumed away from the workplace unless there is reasonable suspicion that consumption during nonworking hours is affecting on-the-job performance.

- No bargaining unit member will be subject to any testing policy or procedure that isn't applied equally to all other employees performing work
of similar sensitivity or impact on public health or safety—including
management and supervisory personnel!

2. *Grounds for Testing*

- Random or universal substance abuse testing is prohibited unless it is
specifically required for the employer by a prior court decision.
- Substance abuse testing in other circumstances is prohibited unless the
employer possesses facts leading to a reasonable basis upon which to
conclude that probable cause exists that an employee is guilty of on-the-
job impairment or possession of illegal drugs.

3. *Test Selection*

- The employer must obtain the union's consent in selecting the type of
test and laboratory facility which will perform the analysis.
- Only laboratories and test products which are routinely inspected and
checked for sensitivity and specificity will be used.
- The union retains to right to demand a change in test product or laboratory based on information which challenges the accuracy or quality of
either, or when a superior alternative to either is available.

4. *Consequences of Testing Positive*

- All samples which initially test positive will be retested using a second
analysis (GC/MS).
- An employee whose test is confirmed positive will be referred to an
EAP before being disciplined.
- Discipline related to a confirmed positive test result shall be progressive
and consistent with the seriousness of the infraction.
- An employee who tests positive shall have the right to challenge the accuracy of the test results before any disciplinary procedure is involved.
To avoid frivolous use of either disciplinary action or grievances, it may
be useful to specify procedures for speedy arbitration of proposed disciplinary actions resulting from alleged substance abuse. For example,
firefighter contracts with the City of Miami and the City of Miami
Beach provide for confirmation of an initial positive test within twenty-
four hours of the initial positive test result and arbitration of proposed
discipline within seventy-two hours thereafter. This meets management's need to manage risks by removing the affected employee from

the job, enabling management and the union's need to protect its members' rights to due process and just cause.[22]

5. *Employee Rights*

- The employee assistance program will be controlled by an advisory board which will include union representation.

- The employee will have the right to union representation during any part of a substance abuse testing process.

- All aspects of a substance abuse testing policy and procedure will be subject to arbitration.

- The employee will be given a sample of his or her own specimen so that a separate test can be administered at the employee's expense, if so desired.

- All test results will be kept confidential and will be available only to a designated employer representative, a designated union representative, or a designated legal representative.

- Any employee who tests positive shall be given access to all written documentation available from the testing laboratory which verifies the accuracy of the equipment, the qualifications of laboratory personnel, the chain of custody of the specimen, and the accuracy rate of the laboratory.

- Any employee who is referred to the EAP for treatment of a substance abuse problem, whether voluntarily or involuntarily, is entitled to full and fair treatment up to the limits provided by the employer's contract with the health care provider.

- Once the union enters into an agreement with management concerning substance abuse testing, it also becomes liable under the constitutional and statutory provisions discussed in Chapter 3. Therefore, the union will conduct itself so as to protect the constitutional or statutory employment rights of its members and fairly represent the interests of all bargaining unit members (whether union members or not) in all grievances and arbitration issues arising out of the implementation of the substance abuse testing program.

SUMMARY

Employees almost universally believe that the employer's first response to employees with a substance abuse problem should be to help the employee. This is regardless of whether the problem is with a legal drug (such as alcohol) or an illegal one. This means that employers who emphasize that alcohol and drug abuse are health and efficiency issues to be dealt with from a medical perspective (at least until it is evident that medical treatment has been unsuccessful) and who follow through on this policy in their personnel practices, are more likely to be able to "sell" themselves to their employees. By continuing to inform employees that help for addiction problems is available through their employer and by providing this help to those employees who seek it, personnel managers are likely to find that more and more employees will favor substance abuse testing.

The employer should carefully and thoroughly train supervisors to manage for productivity, recognize the indicators of a performance problem, adequately document performance discrepancies, and effectively counsel employees with performance problems.

The employer should freely share information with the union about proposed substance abuse testing policies and procedures. It should solicit union help in implementing the program and "selling" it to employees.

NOTES

1. Miners, I., & Nykodym, N. (1986, August). Put drug detection to the test. *Personnel Journal, 13*(8), p. 39.

2. Sexton, T., & Zilz, U. On the wisdom of mandatory drug testing. *Journal of Policy Analysis and Management, 7*(3), pp. 542–564; and Gomez-Mejia, L., & Balkin, D. (1987). Dimensions and characteristics of personnel manager perceptions of effective drug-testing programs. *Personnel Psychology, 40*, pp. 745–763.

3. O'Keefe, A. (1987, June). The case against drug testing. *Psychology Today*, pp. 199–201.

4. Mensch, B., & Kandel, D. (1988, June). Do job conditions influence the use of drugs? *Journal of Health and Social Behavior, 29*, pp. 169–184.

5. Crowley, J. (1985). *The demographics of alcohol use among young Americans: Results from the 1983 national longitudinal survey of labor market experience of youth.* Columbus, OH: Center for Human Resource Research, The Ohio State University.

6. Hollinger, R. (1988). Working under the influence (WUI): Correlates of employees' use of alcohol and other drugs. *The Journal of Applied Behavioral Science, 24*(4), pp. 439–454.

7. Ames, G. (1989, Fall). Alcohol-related movements and the effects on drinking policies in the American workplace: An historical review. *Journal of Drug Issues*, pp. 489–509.

8. Klingner, D., Culp, M., Freeman, B., Jensen, T., & Stevenson, R. (1989, October 31). *Drug use and attitude survey of selected employers in Dade County, Florida.* Miami, FL: Miami Coalition for a Drug Free Community, Report of the Scientific Advisory Workplace Drug Survey Subcommittee.

9. While, H., Aidala, A., & Zablocki, B. (1988). A longitudinal investigation of work patterns among middle-class, white adults. *The Journal of Applied Behavioral Science, 24*(4), pp. 455–469.

10. Alexander, B. (1990, Winter). Alternatives to the war on drugs. *Journal of Drug Issues, 20*(1), pp. 7–8.

11. Klingner, D., & Nalbandian, J. (1985). *Public personnel management: Contexts and strategies.* Englewood Cliffs, NJ: Prentice-Hall, 2nd edition.

12. Jansen, M. (1986). Emotional disorders and the labour force. *International Labour Review, 125*(5), pp. 605–615.

13. See, for example, Masters, M., Farris, G., & Ratcliff, S. (1988, July). Practices and attitudes of substance abuse testing. *Personnel Administrator, 33*, pp. 72–79; Smith, B. (1988, October). Employee-supported drug testing. *Personnel Journal, 67*, pp. 134–137; and Hanson, D. (1988, June). Drug abuse testing programs gaining acceptance in workplace. *Chemical & Engineering News, 64*, pp. 7–15.

14. Markowitz, M. (1987, December). The organization and employee alcohol misuse. *Human Relations, 40*, pp. 833–851.

15. Bottorff, S. (1986, December 10). ACLU charges bias in hospital drug testing. *The Los Angeles Daily Journal*, Section II, p. 1.

16. Harris, M., & Fennell, M. (1988). Perceptions of an employee assistance program and employees' willingness to participate. *The Journal of Applied Behavioral Science, 24*(4), pp. 423–438.

17. Pace, L. (1989, July). When managers themselves are substance abusers. *Personnel Journal, 68*, pp. 70–72.

18. Klingner, D., & Nalbandian, J. (1985). *Public personnel management: Contexts and strategies*. Englewood Cliffs, NJ: Prentice-Hall, 2nd edition.

19. Jar wars: Drug testing and your rights. (1986, November-December). *Public Employee, 51*(8).

20. Masters, M. (1988). The negotiability of drug testing in the federal sector: A political perspective. *The Journal of Collective Negotiations in the Public Sector, 17*(4), pp. 309–325; and Aron, M. (1987, March). Drug testing: The employer's dilemma. *Labor Law Journal*, pp. 157–165.

21. Conlan, K. (1986, November 26). *Workplace drug testing: A union reference guide for policy making*. Washington, D.C.: Workplace Economics, Inc., Section 6, pp. 8–11.

22. Article 30, Substance/alcohol—personal screening.

Part II
AIDS Testing

7

The Problem of AIDS

AIDS is a worldwide health problem which has reached epidemic proportions in developing countries. The World Health Organization now estimates that 8–10 million people are infected with the AIDS virus[1] and that 15–20 million will be infected by the year 2000. It regards these figures as conservative estimates.

AIDS was first reported in the United States in 1981. Since that time, the U.S. Public Health Service has received reports that almost 152,000 persons have contracted AIDS, and over half of them have died of the disease.[2] It is currently estimated that 1.5 million people have the virus, of whom about 30 percent can be expected to contract AIDS.

AIDS is a progressive disease. Although there are drugs that will slow its advance or prevent those persons carrying the virus from developing symptoms of the disease itself, the disease is invariably fatal once the victim's immune system has been destroyed. Although there is an increasing rate of heterosexual transmission, AIDS is transmitted primarily by unsafe homosexual practices (primarily anal intercourse among gay males), needle sharing by intravenous drug addicts, transfusions of blood from infected donors, and transmission in the uterus from infected mothers to their infants.

The health care costs of AIDS are enormous. Early studies estimated $61,000–$94,000 per person from onset to death, but these figures were based on a brief lifespan from onset to death (1–3 years), and extensive use of volunteer patient care providers from within the gay community. As AIDS is detected earlier and patients survive longer, lifespan estimates have now increased (7–10 years). And the magnitude of the AIDS epidemic has increased far beyond the abilities of volunteer social service agencies to provide treatment for AIDS patients. This means that health care providers must be increasingly used, at a far greater cost.[3] And AIDS is a workplace issue because it strikes a segment of the population normally exempt from costly, fatal diseases (otherwise healthy males and females between 25 and 45).

The workplace implications of AIDS are tremendous. The risk of workplace transmission is almost nonexistent (except for health care workers whose job duties involve the possibility of blood-to-blood contact). But the health care costs are so high that human resource managers are concerned about hiring applicants with AIDS. And the public's hysteria about the moral stigma of the disease means that personnel directors must carefully consider the issue from the viewpoint of those who have the disease, and those concerned about catching it.

OBJECTIVES

The purpose of this chapter is to:

1. Review the problem of Acquired Immune Deficiency Syndrome (AIDS) in our society, from a social, economic, legal, and political perspective.

2. Evaluate why AIDS has taken so long to emerge as a public policy issue at the national level and why it is finally doing so now.

3. Describe the public policy measures now being taken to stop the spread of AIDS.

4. Examine the particular impact of AIDS in the workplace, both for those employees who have AIDS (productivity, liability, and health care costs) and for their co-workers and clients.

5. Introduce the general strategies used by employers to deal with these issues.

THE PROBLEM OF AIDS

What Is AIDS?

AIDS (Acquired Immune Deficiency Syndrome) is a fatal disease caused by a virus. In the first stage of the disease, the only sign of infection is a positive blood test to the antibodies which the body produces in an effort to destroy the HIV (Human Immunodeficiency Virus). The virus itself is not the direct cause of death.

Rather, it brings about a suppression of the white blood cells that would normally be able to fight certain disease entities which ultimately cause death in the AIDS patient.

Because AIDS has been researched for less than a decade, medical experts are uncertain what percentage of persons who carry the AIDS virus will eventually develop further symptoms of AIDS.[4] While some experts conclude that 30 percent of AIDS carriers will do so, other estimates and projections indicate that almost all of the male homosexuals now infected with the AIDS virus will eventually die of AIDS if they do not die first of other causes.[5]

But regardless of these differences, they do agree that the first stage of AIDS is extremely dangerous. People infected with the AIDS virus (HIV) who show no active symptoms of the disease may still spread it to others through unprotected sexual contact, sharing of intravenous needles, and transmission to the unborn fetus during pregnancy or childbirth.

While it is believed that everyone who carries the AIDS virus can transmit it to others, only about 30 percent of those persons develop the progressively more severe symptoms of ARC (AIDS-Related Complex) or "full-blown" AIDS. The extent to which AIDS progresses and the rate of progression are determined by whether (and how quickly) the AIDS virus destroys the body's natural immune system by attacking and destroying the white blood cells (T-leucocytes) which keep persons healthy by routinely destroying diseases in the bloodstream.

In a healthy individual, there are about 950 T-cells per cubic milliliter of blood. When this number drops below 400, the HIV-positive person (one carrying the HIV) is quite vulnerable to opportunistic diseases—flu, colds, fungi, and protozoa—which would not be life-threatening to a healthy person. This susceptibility to opportunistic infections is called ARC, or AIDS-Related Complex. Among its characteristics are weight loss, infections of the lymphatic system, fever, or diarrhea.

If AIDS is detected before the onset of ARC, or soon enough thereafter so that the immune system can still function, drugs (such as AZT—azidothymidine) may prolong the life of the patient for several years. AZT was originally marketed by Burroughs Wellcome at an annual cost of $10,000 per patient per year. However, the annual cost has now decreased to about $3,000 per year due to the application of political pressure on the manufacturer by AIDS patients and a downward revision of the dosage (to approximately half the original recommended by the manufacturer) resulting from clinical findings that lower doses were equally effective. In addition, many public health agencies and AIDS treatment networks subsidize the cost of the medication. However, even though $3,000 per patient per year is a relatively low figure in comparison with the cost of treating ARC or full-blown AIDS, it is a sufficiently high figure to be beyond the means of many AIDS victims. Thus, the allocation of public funds for purchase of AZT poses a public health resource dilemma.

Once the body's immune system has been destroyed ("full-blown AIDS"), death is inevitable.

How Is AIDS Transmitted?

The only known means of being infected by the AIDS virus are through sexual contact with infected persons, through the injection of infected blood (in a transfusion or through the sharing of needles among intravenous drug users), or between mother and child during pregnancy and breastfeeding. And sexual transmission is most likely to occur during anal intercourse between gay males because the tearing of the anal tissue allows semen from an infected person to directly enter the bloodstream of his sex partner.

Therefore, it is extremely important to understand that *the risk of AIDS is not related to genetic factors or sexual preference*. That is, members of certain groups (such as Haitians or male homosexuals) are *not* more likely than others to contract AIDS. Rather, the risk of AIDS is based solely on the practices described above. Any group can be at risk if the members of the group choose behavior patterns that are known to increase the susceptibility to AIDS.

The risk of accidental transmission of AIDS through a transfusion of infected blood is extremely rare. In 1985, when 8,000 cases of AIDS had already been documented, only 106 were linked to transfusions, even though 10 million to 12 million units of blood are administered each year.[6]

Although the AIDS virus is fatal, it cannot survive outside the human body. Although traces of the AIDS virus are present in other body fluids (such as tears or saliva), they are not present in strong enough concentrations to be transmitted. Because the AIDS virus is destroyed by digestive juices, the virus also cannot be transmitted through eating or drinking substances tainted with semen or blood from AIDS carriers. AIDS can only be transmitted by direct exchange of blood or semen from an infected person to someone else.

AIDS cannot be transmitted by any form of casual, nonsexual contact between infected and noninfected persons. Nor can it be spread environmentally (for example, by mosquitoes who bite both infected and noninfected persons). It cannot be spread by doorknobs, toilet seats, telephones, office equipment, glasses, utensils, or other objects. Nor is it transmitted through saliva, tears, nasal secretions, urine, or feces.

Therefore, because the means of transmission are known and limited, it is possible to prevent the spread of AIDS by stopping its transmission.

How Widespread Is AIDS?

Over 1.5 million persons in the United States now carry the AIDS virus. Many have no symptoms. Almost 100,000 cases have been reported by July 1989, the latest date for which estimates are available; over 50,000 have died already.[7] Authorities estimate that more than 300,000 persons will have developed AIDS by 1992,[8] and 180,000 will have died. For 1991 alone, a death rate of 54,000 is predicted.[9]

Most reported cases of AIDS are in New York and California, followed by Florida, Texas, New Jersey, Illinois, Pennsylvania, Massachusetts, Georgia, and the

Table 6
Race and Ethnicity of Persons with AIDS in the United States

	White	Black	Hispanic
Men who have sex with other men	75%	15%	10%
Intravenous drug users	19	51	30
Both of the above	65	22	13
Heterosexual cases	14	72	13
Blood clotting disorders	86	5	7
Transfusion recipients	77	14	7
Undetermined	37	42	19
Children with AIDS	20	55	24

District of Columbia. The cities where AIDS is most common are New York (28 percent of cases), San Francisco (10 percent), and Los Angeles (8 percent), followed by Houston, Washington, Miami, Newark, Chicago, Dallas, Philadelphia, and Boston.[10] Initially, AIDS cases were concentrated among members of those groups which tended to engage in the practices placing them at increased risk of AIDS transmission—male homosexuals and intravenous drug users. Currently, almost 90 percent of all AIDS victims fall within these groups[11] (see Tables 6[12] and 7[13]).

But increasingly and inevitably, AIDS is spreading from these groups into the general population through their sex partners and children.[14]

Several factors make it difficult to determine exactly how many people have AIDS—the nature of the disease, the moral stigma attached to it, and the invisible nature of many carriers. First, the nature of the disease is such that persons can carry the virus for a long time without experiencing any symptoms. In this respect, AIDS is similar to any number of other diseases (such as high blood pressure or diabetes). Thus, they are not likely to bring themselves to the attention of a doctor or a public health agency.

Second, the massive public education effort designed to allay public panic about the "AIDS epidemic" has made people more aware that (unlike these other diseases) AIDS is not transmitted genetically or environmentally, but as a result of behaviors which are known and can be prevented. Also unlike these other diseases, it is fatal for a high percentage (current estimates predict that about 30 percent of AIDS virus carriers will develop "full-blown" AIDS or ARC) of its carriers, and transmittable to their sex partners (the risk of transmission is highest for anal intercourse and lower for vaginal intercourse). This has had the effect of making those who suspect they may have AIDS less likely to voluntarily undergo testing or to divulge the results. And those who carry the AIDS virus may have it for at least six months prior to testing positive.[15] During this time they may unwittingly transmit the virus to others. The fact that an increasing number of children are born with AIDS as a result of behavior by their parents for which the newborn child could not by any stretch of the imagination be considered responsible may result in a diminished tendency by the public to blame the victims of AIDS rather than to address it as a public health policy issue.

Table 7
Gender of Persons with AIDS in the United States

	Male	Female
Men who have sex with other men	100%	n/a
Intravenous drug users	79	21
Both of the above	100	n/a
Heterosexual cases	48	52
Blood clotting disorders	98	2
Transfusion recipients	64	36
Undetermined	78	22
Children with AIDS	55	45

Third, the most likely vectors for the spread of AIDS into the general population are large but socially "invisible"—intravenous drug users and male homosexuals and bisexuals. The increase in our prison population due to drug convictions has concentrated intravenous drug users in a situation where "unsafe sex" (anal intercourse without condoms) is the rule rather than the exception. Given that almost all inmates (who are encouraged by prison conditions to share needles and engage in unsafe sex) are at some time released back into the general population, it does not seem possible that AIDS can be prevented from moving gradually through most of the population.

These three factors make it difficult to determine conclusively what the incidence is of AIDS in the general population. The federal Centers for Disease Control estimates are based on projections of the number of homosexuals, drug abusers, and others who are most likely to be infected. Studies from other groups, using other methods, have reached widely differing conclusions, ranging from half to more than *double* the federal agency's figure.[16]

Tests of newborn infants' blood in inner-city hospitals in major metropolitan areas indicate that the AIDS virus is more widespread among young women of childbearing age than previous studies had suggested. While early studies showed that 0.2 percent of the women who gave birth at fifty-eight hospitals had the AIDS virus,[17] current estimates for high-risk women in inner-city hospitals are up to *twenty times higher* than those previously reported for females or the general population. And even these figures may be low, because babies born with the AIDS virus may not test positive for six months after birth.

The reality is that AIDS researchers and epidemiologists are hampered by a general lack of knowledge about human sexual behavior. We don't know the age at which people begin sexual activity, the frequency with which they change partners, or their specific sexual practices. Efforts to determine this information have often been hampered by political considerations.[18]

Treating Patients with AIDS

AIDS is a fatal disease, in that a high percentage of those who carry the AIDS virus have died of it or will die of it. But early detection and treatment can prolong the lives and diminish the suffering of AIDS patients considerably. For example, in 1983, before doctors and hospitals were alert to the symptoms of AIDS, most patients died within a year of diagnosis. Now patients can considerably extend their lives by maintaining their body weight, eating and exercising regularly, avoiding opportunistic infections (such as pneumonia and tuberculosis), and taking new drugs (such as AZT, marketed by Burroughs Wellcome pharmaceutical company under the trade name Retrovir) which place the disease in remission by permanently blocking the destruction of the white blood cells by the AIDS virus. Therefore, the patient is better able to fight off the opportunistic diseases that constitute the ARC. This means that while AIDS cannot be cured at present, early detection and treatment (including AZT) can prolong the life of AIDS patients indefinitely, or at least for many years.

While many laboratories are working to develop a vaccine against the AIDS virus, it is uncertain how quickly one can be developed, tested, and marketed.[19] For example, it took almost fifteen years for the vaccine for hepatitis B to be marketed after it was developed. And the constant stream of newspaper reports about the development of AIDS vaccines must be viewed with caution—the intensity of the public's interest in AIDS treatment renders us vulnerable to stock price manipulations for biotech firms based on press releases rather than replicable scientific findings.[20]

WHY HAS AIDS EMERGED SO SLOWLY AS A PUBLIC POLICY ISSUE?

Until recently, there were no signs of any clear public policy to restrict the spread of AIDS.[21] This was due to four major factors. First, issues of confidentiality have hampered our ability to determine how widespread AIDS is and therefore our ability to develop programs designed to identify, educate, and treat carriers of the virus. Second, there has been widespread ignorance and denial of the critical role of our prison system in spreading AIDS throughout the general population. Third, it was possible for the general population to deny the threat of AIDS for a long time because the groups most affected by it (minority male homosexuals and intravenous drug users) were already invisible politically and socially. And these three, taken together, led to a fourth reason. With the exception of the pioneering role of the CDC in monitoring the progress of the disease during the 1980s, the federal government did not get seriously involved in AIDS treatment as a national public health issue until 1990.

Confidentiality Makes Accurate Data Scarce

The stigma attached to AIDS and the rights to privacy of patients tested for the virus mean that it is very difficult to get accurate and complete data on the number of persons who are infected with the AIDS virus or who have died of AIDS. First, patient confidentiality means that under applicable state laws, physicians are not always required to advise state public health services if a person tests positive for the AIDS virus.[22] This in turn means that the CDC (which obtains its figures from these state reports) must base its predictions of infection rates on incomplete data or population estimates rather than actual infection reports. Second, the fact that AIDS victims do not die of AIDS but of a variety of opportunistic diseases which attack the victim once immunity is suppressed means that the actual number of AIDS deaths may be underreported because of pressure by victims' families on the physician who signs the death certificate to give the cause of death as something else (such as pneumonia).

Therefore, our best estimates of the incidence of AIDS come from mandatory testing of high-risk populations (prisoners) or random testing of aggregate populations (such as newborns). It is difficult for public officials to accurately estimate how many persons have AIDS and for health care professionals to identify, treat, and educate individuals who carry the AIDS virus so as to prevent them from spreading it.

And the use of aggregate data also raises serious ethical issues. If the confidentiality of patient records is protected through the release of aggregate data only, this may prevent the early detection and treatment of AIDS in the individual patient. For example, if newborns are tested for AIDS and their confidentiality is maintained through the release of only aggregate data, does not this deprive the baby's parents and physician of the right to know that the newborn has AIDS, so that treatment can be initiated which might save or prolong the baby's life?

Prisons Spread AIDS

The real problem with transmission of AIDS into the general population is our prison system. Our efforts to reduce the impact of drugs on society have resulted in tremendous increases in arrests, prosecutions, and prison time for drug offenders. For example, the state prison population has increased from 330,000 in 1981 to 650,000 in 1989.[23] The vast majority of the increase is of drug-related offenders. Even if we could afford to do so, we cannot build prisons fast enough to keep up with the demand. This means that prisons are overcrowded, that their budgets are tight, and that their medical facilities are inadequate to cope with normal medical conditions (much less AIDS or AIDS-related infections). Prisons contribute to AIDS because they concentrate together persons who are likely to be carriers of the virus, in an environment which encourages those practices most conducive to the spread of AIDS.

The experience of the New York State prison system is that inmates with AIDS are not hospitalized until they are very sick or even dying. They live only half as long as persons with AIDS on the outside.[24] Information from New York City's prison system indicates that 115,000 persons per year are incarcerated at Rikers Island, the city's largest prison. Many of these are convicted drug offenders. About 25 percent of these persons test positive for AIDS. Homosexuality is widespread in prison, yet the prison system has not used this opportunity to teach inmates about safe sex or to provide inmates with condoms, because many critics feel that to do so would be tacit encouragement of homosexuality by inmates.

The result is that our prison system functions as an incredibly effective mechanism for spreading AIDS throughout society. Inmates are concentrated together in a setting where they are likely to contract AIDS or pass it to others. They are then released back into society when they have served their sentences, to pass the virus on to their sex partners or other drug addicts through the sharing of needles. This does not mean they are rehabilitated—studies show uniformly that recidivism rates increase directly with the extent of contact the individual has had with the criminal justice system. But the cell is needed for someone else who has just been convicted and sentenced.

The medical director of New York State's prison system has requested an additional $50 million for AIDS detection and treatment in the prison system. He knows he won't get it. He is extremely pessimistic about the likelihood of reducing the spread of AIDS before its high costs overwhelm our public health system. In the short run, the likely policy option is going to be that the system authorizes a medical clemency policy to release terminally ill AIDS patients back into society so that they can obtain better medical care than is available in the prisons, spend time with their families, and die in a fashion that does not take resources from the already overwhelmed prison medical system.

But necessary as this may be for the prison system, and humane as it may be for individual inmates, it is also likely to increase the diffusion of AIDS to the general population. An AIDS patient due to die within a month from "full-blown" AIDS poses no risk for transmission. But a patient with some symptoms of ARC may go into remission if provided with AZT and other treatments, at least for a sufficient period to enable transmission of the disease to others through unsafe sex or needle sharing. This means that prison medical directors face an impossible dilemma. Their choices are to withhold humanitarian release of AIDS patients until they are very near death (and face intense public criticism from patients, their families, and AIDS interest groups for denying victims' rights for treatment), or to release AIDS victims early enough for them to prolong life through better treatment (and face intense public criticism from corrections officials, public health experts, and the general public for exposing the public to increased threat of AIDS transmission).

In sum, both drugs and AIDS are societal issues which have become workplace problems. But the public policy measures we have adopted to fight the war on drugs from a legal and moral perspective are quite likely to make us lose the war on AIDS from a public health viewpoint. In fact, we could not have done a better job at designing legal and correctional policies guaranteed to spread AIDS from its primary population (intravenous drug users and male homosexuals) into the general population.

High-Risk Groups Are Invisible

Currently, AIDS claims far fewer lives annually than heart attacks, smoking, or automobile accidents. But it is a much more explosive health problem because it is invariably fatal, costly, and morally repugnant because of the dominant society's view of the primary ways it is transmitted. These conditions mean that the general public is likely to have a low level of understanding of AIDS and a high anxiety level about the disease. Therefore, people can be expected to avoid determining whether they have AIDS, or if they do, to avoid learning information or making changes in their behavior that would result in a reduced transmission rate for the disease.

The realization that they are likely to die from AIDS may make AIDS victims indifferent to their own health or that of others they may infect.[25] For example, a 1988 study reported that only 473 of the estimated 14,000 intravenous drug users in the greater Boston area identified themselves for anonymous testing and counseling.[26] In addition, the Dallas Seroprevalence Study found far fewer persons with AIDS than predicted in Dallas County, but 205 of the 1,446 people included in the sample refused to provide a blood sample. And the rate of positive tests for those who initially refused to provide a sample but later did so was much higher than the rate of positive tests for those who initially consented to provide a blood sample.[27]

What's worse, many of those who know they are infected with AIDS deliberately avoid taking precautions. They are afraid and angry and choose to respond by trying to give AIDS to others. In a recent incident exemplifying this response, a male homosexual prostitute in Los Angeles was acquitted of charges of twice selling his blood to a private blood center even though he knew he was infected with AIDS.

It is understandable that we have ignored the link between our criminal justice policies for eradication of substance abuse and our public health policies for stopping the spread of AIDS. The high-risk groups are already marginalized into invisible or deviant behavior patterns reflecting their lack of social, economic, and political power. Therefore they are invisible, and our public policy debates tend either to ignore them or focus on ways of limiting their impact on the larger society.

Without a clear understanding of how their values and feelings give rise to the antisocial behaviors which spread AIDS and the conditions that give rise to these values and feelings, we will continue to see them as part of the problem. And as long as this is our attitude, we will not be able to constructively involve them in solving it.

The Federal Government Has Not Been Involved

Taken together, these three factors have meant that AIDS treatment has been ignored as a national public health or public policy issue until 1990. Until recently, AIDS was the first epidemic in recent American history to be fought almost entirely by states and local communities.[28] The same pattern of denial and panic that characterizes the individual's response to AIDS also seemed, at least until recently, to be present at a national public policy level.[29] Because five states (New York, California, Texas, Florida, and New Jersey) have over 70 percent of the AIDS cases, both policy initiatives and funding have been concentrated in these states.

And some of these efforts seem counterproductive. For example, Louisiana recently mandated AIDS tests at the individual's expense for couples seeking marriage licenses. Yet experts agree that this is a low-risk group, for which the inevitable rate of false positives would pose a far greater problem than the opportunities for education and counseling resulting from detection of persons actually infected with AIDS.

The Federal Government Enters the Picture

The result of these conditions has been that moral and religious concerns have posed serious social and political barriers to prevention of the epidemic, hampering scientific efforts to learn enough about how AIDS has spread and blocking effective steps to slow it. Now, at last, there are some signs that the federal government is ready to address AIDS as a national public health crisis. In February 1989, the National Academy of Sciences recommended that the federal government test every newborn baby in America for AIDS, give drug addicts clean needles, and require broadcast media to accept advertisements for condoms.[30] Each of these recommendations has been supported by considerable research. But adoption as public health objectives has been slower because of the value conflicts involved.

Aggregate testing of some newborns (primarily in public hospitals) is already occurring in forty-four states. And traditional public health practices such as contact tracing can be adapted for tracing the spread of AIDS. Traditionally, public health workers have attempted to halt the spread of syphilis and other venereal diseases by asking infected persons to identify their sexual contacts and then contacting each of these persons to advise them that they may have contracted a venereal disease. In this manner, persons who may be infected can obtain prompt treatment before they have the chance to spread the disease widely themselves.

In the case of AIDS, this traditional procedure was not followed because the social stigma of the disease warranted confidentiality for its victims and because of the belief that infected persons would not identify sexual contacts for fear of ostracism or retaliation. But two factors have changed this: increased realization of the need to stop the spread of AIDS before it exhausts all our public health resources and increased awareness that, while AIDS cannot presently be cured, its effects can be slowed or halted if it is discovered and treatment begun quickly.

For example, recent research shows that programs to give intravenous drug users clean needles or to show them how to sterilize their own needles with bleach do not increase the intravenous drug use.[31] But street outreach programs to accomplish these objectives continue to be illegal under federal law, and they have encountered intense public criticism in areas where they have been tried on an experimental basis. In addition, they require cultural sensitivity and depend on our ability to reverse the prevalent pattern of marginalizing (avoiding and ignoring) the behavior patterns of intravenous drug users and their sex partners.[32]

Lastly, there is a much greater degree of public acceptance that preventing the exchange of body fluids (blood and semen) by using condoms is an effective means

of reducing the spread of AIDS from infected persons to their sex partners. While traditional religious spokesmen may object to condoms as a birth control method or to their distribution in prisons on the grounds that to do so would be to condone illegal behavior, these voices are a distinct minority. Condoms and other contraceptive methods are today widely advertised in newspapers, on television, in college magazines, and health clinics. They are often available free through student health services.

AIDS and the Workplace

AIDS is beginning to be a workplace problem for two distinct groups of employees. First, the group that runs some risk of contracting AIDS are the health care workers whose jobs involve working with the body fluids of AIDS patients (physicians, nurses, laboratory technicians, paramedics, and some police officers). There is a slight chance that one of these workers can become infected through an accidental needle stick from a syringe containing blood from an infected person or by blood from an infected person entering the employee's bloodstream through a cut. Although patients may have a strong reaction to being treated by a health care worker who has AIDS, there is no possibility that AIDS can be transmitted except by blood-to-blood contact. However, there is a possibility that other opportunistic infections to which the AIDS victim is susceptible may be transmitted from employees to patients through workplace contact, especially to patients whose immune systems may be weakened by the conditions for which they are hospitalized.

The second group is composed of those employees who have AIDS victims among their co-workers. And while these employees are in no danger of contracting AIDS from a co-worker, the fear and denial that AIDS generates among employees and their families can cause the issue to give rise to serious personnel problems. Employees (or their union representatives) can demand that employees with the AIDS virus be identified and isolated or discharged so as to prevent them from infecting others, even if there is no chance of the infection being transmitted in the course of job duties. Employees with the AIDS virus can demand confidentiality and the right not to be discriminated against in personnel actions on the basis of a handicap as long as they can continue to do their jobs.

Thus, AIDS generates increased concern among employers about liability risks and employee productivity. But these are relatively simple issues to address. Liability risks for contracting AIDS can be greatly reduced (for that small group of employees whose jobs require it) by developing protective policies to minimize the risk of exchanging body fluids. Liability issues for other positions can be dealt with by educating employees about the impossibility of contracting AIDS in the workplace. Concerns for productivity can be met by developing clear policies designed to determine whether an AIDS carrier can perform the duties of the position. The desired outcome is a balanced approach reflecting the employer's desire to make reasonable accommodation to the AIDS victim while this person is still healthy enough to perform the primary duties of the position, and to clarify policies with respect to sick leave, disability retirement, and dependent benefits once the person is forced by failing health to leave the work force.

But tremendous pressure is being exerted on employers by the health insurance industry. Obviously, it is in the insurers' best interest to identify carriers of the AIDS virus prior to employment and to have AIDS or AIDS-related diseases excluded from coverage as pre-existing conditions. Similarly, it is in the employer's best interest to do so if the agency is self-insured. And this causes a fundamental conflict between the values of individual rights (both for AIDS victims and their co-workers) and efficiency (defined as reduced health care costs and employee productivity). And liability issues are critical here as well, in that violations of either value can give rise to a costly lawsuit.

The traditional response of employers to this dilemma has been identical to the response of individuals and public policy-makers—first denial, then panic, and last the development of clear and reasonable policies. And health and life insurance companies are taking the lead in spurring their corporate and agency clients to move quickly from denial to policymaking in this area.

The New England Corporate Consortium for AIDS Education, a leadership and advocacy group of nine Boston-area businesses that promotes workplace education about AIDS, recently presented the U.S. headquarters of Sun Life Assurance Company of Canada with an award for its outstanding contribution to and leadership in this new field.[33] With the help of AIDS Action Committee of Massachussetts, Inc., a nonprofit advocacy and education group in Boston, Sun Life recently implemented an in-house AIDS educational program for its employees and managers. The program includes:

- information about how AIDS is contracted;
- instruction for managers in handling employees with AIDS and the legal implications of dealing with these employees;
- training an employee to run ongoing AIDS education programs.

Paul Ross, the group's chairman, said that only 10 percent of U.S. employers formally address AIDS in the workplace. According to him, "The clear message is, from our perspective, this is going to be the employee relations issue of the 1990s. Get started now—don't wait for your first AIDS case, because people will panic."[34]

SUMMARY

AIDS (Acquired Immune Deficiency Syndrome) is an opportunistic, fatal disease which is gradually spreading from its initial population (male homosexuals and intravenous drug users) into the general population. Ironically, the spread of AIDS into the general population in the United States is one unanticipated result of the increased imprisonment of drug-involved criminals as a result of the war on drugs.

The emergence of AIDS as a national public policy issue has taken a long time, since the first cases were identified in the United States in 1981. This is due to problems with identifying carriers, conflicts between public health needs and the objectives of our correctional system, and the moral and social stigma attached to the disease itself. Hopefully, this is now changing, as a massive infusion of federal aid coalesces behind continuing efforts to reduce the spread of AIDS through more research, better public education, and more cohesive federal policy.[35]

As a workplace issue, AIDS is beginning to be of critical importance because of its implications for productivity and liability. But most of all, the potentially huge losses it places on health insurance carriers or self-insured employers means that it brings two fundamental values into open conflict. Under penalty of lawsuit for violation of handicap protection laws, applicants and employees who carry the AIDS virus have the right to a job as long as they can perform its primary duties with reasonable modifications by the employer. But no employer or health insurance carrier would make a voluntary, rational decision to employ an applicant knowing that this person would only live a few more years and would cost the employer $100,000–$250,000 in health care from onset until death.

Employers are only now beginning to address this dilemma. They are being urged to do so by health and life insurance companies, which are confronted by this dilemma right now. Hopefully, the result will be the development of AIDS policies by employers and increased education of employees and managers.[36]

NOTES

1. HIV infection worldwide estimated at 8–10 million. (1990, August 31). *AIDS Update*, p. 6.

2. Makadon, H., Seage III, F., Thorpe, K., & Fineberg, H. (1990). Paying the medical cost of the HIV epidemic: A review of policy options. *Journal of Acquired Immune Deficiency Syndromes, 3*, pp. 123–133.

3. Ibid.

4. Volberding, P. (1989). HIV infection as a disease: The medical indications for early diagnosis. *Journal of Acquired Immune Deficiency Syndromes, 2*, pp. 421–425.

5. 99% of gay men infected will get AIDS. (1988, June 2). *The Miami Herald*, p. 7A.

6. Clark, M., with Abrams, P. (1985, July 13). AIDS: the blood bank scare. *Newsweek*, p. 47.

7. Makadon, H., et al. (1990). Paying the medical cost.

8. Weyward, W., & Curran, J. (1988). The epidemiology of AIDS in the U.S. *Scientific American, 259*, pp. 72–81.

9. The facts about AIDS: A special NEA higher education advocate report. (1988). *Higher Education Advocate*. Washington, D.C.: National Education Association, p. 2.

10. Ibid., p. 5.

11. Turk, H. (1989, Spring). AIDS: The first decade. *Employee Relations Law Journal, 14*(4), pp. 531–547.

12. The facts about AIDS, p. 5.

13. Ibid., p. 5.

14. Palca, J. (1990). AIDS and the future. *Science, 248*, p. 1484.

15. Heacock, M., & Orvis, G. (1990). AIDS in the workplace: Public and corporate policy. *Harvard Journal of Law & Public Policy, 13*(2), p. 702

16. Belkin, L. (1990, May 12). Questions on AIDS figures emerge from Dallas survey. *The New York Times*, p. Y-6.

17. Halpert, D. (1989, February 29). Test babies for AIDS, scientists urge. *The Miami Herald*, pp. 1A, 23A.

18. Brown, P. (1990, May). Is sex too important to keep quiet about? *New Scientist, 2*, pp. 28–29.

19. Brown, P. (1990, May). French institute claims progress with AIDS vaccine. *New Scientist, 5*, p. 24.

20. Stocks on seesaw after a flurry of AIDS news releases. (1990, July 8). *The Miami Herald*, pp. 1C–2C.

21. Panem, S. (1988). *The AIDS bureaucracy*. Cambridge, MA: Harvard University Press.

22. Gostin, L. (1990, April 11). The AIDS litigation project: A national review of court and human rights commission decisions, part I: The social impact of AIDS. *Journal of the American Medical Association, 263*(14), pp. 1961–1970.

23. Bulging prison populations overwhelm reform efforts. (1990, May 20). *The New York Times*, pp. 1, 18.

24. *AIDS Quarterly*. (1990, May 23). Television series produced and sponsored by the Robert Wood Johnson Foundation.

25. Ohi, G., Hasegawa, T., Kai, I., Inaba, Y., Miyama, T., Kobayashi, M., Muramatsu, Y., Ashizawa, M., Uemura, I., & Nimi, T. (1988, October 12). Notification of HIV carriers: Possible effect on uptake of AIDS testing. *The Lancet, 2*, pp. 947–949.

26. Counseling and testing intravenous drug users for HIV infection. (1988, August 12). *The Journal of the American Medical Association, 282*, pp. 892.

27. Belkin, L. (1990, May 12). Questions on AIDS figures emerge from Dallas survey. *The New York Times*, p. Y-6.

28. Randal, J., & Hines, W. (1987, November). Local communities take the lead in coping with AIDS. *Governing*, pp. 34–40.

29. Joyce, C. (1990, May). U.S. 'failing to combat AIDS,' Bush told. *New Scientist, 5*, p. 23.

30. Halpert, D. (1989, February 23). Test babies for AIDS, scientists urge. *The Miami Herald*, pp. 1A, 23A.

31. Ibid.

32. Conviser, R., & Rutledge, J. (1989). Can public policies limit the spread of HIV among IV drug users? *The Journal of Drug Issues, 19*(1), pp. 113–128.

33. Woolsey, C. (1990, January 8). AIDS effort praised: Life insurer called leader in workplace education. *Business Insurance*, pp. 2, 4.

34. Ibid., p. 2.

35. Barinaga, M. (1990, June). AIDS meeting: Unexpected progress. *New Scientist, 248*, pp. 1596–1597.

36. Makadon, H., et al. (1990). Paying the medical cost.

8

The Technology of AIDS Testing

If substance abuse testing is the human resource management issue of the present, AIDS testing is the human resource management issue of the future. While the problem is not yet a critical one for employers, they are being urged by employee benefit carriers to develop clear policies. And this is occurring against a backdrop of increased public awareness and public policy focus.

Understanding the implications of AIDS testing for employers requires that we familiarize ourselves with the tests used to detect AIDS by detecting the presence of AIDS virus antibodies.

OBJECTIVES

The purpose of this chapter is to:

1. Describe the tests used to detect whether a person is a carrier of the AIDS virus.

2. Evaluate their validity, reliability, and cost.

AIDS TESTING TECHNIQUES

There is no test for diagnosing AIDS. However, there is a test which detects antibodies to the virus that causes AIDS. Antibodies are substances produced by the white blood cells to fight disease organisms. The presence of antibodies to the AIDS virus means that a person has been infected with that virus.

In AIDS testing, an enzyme immuno-assay (EIA) test is the initial step.[1] The EIA test is used to screen donated blood to prevent the transmission of the AIDS virus through blood transfusions. It is also available through private physicians, local AIDS service organizations, and state and local public health services.

Blood samples that test positive are subjected to a second confirmatory test called the Western blot. This test looks at core antigens rather than viral antibodies.

Other Testing Techniques

Because of the public's fear about AIDS, med-tech corporations are busily developing alternative tests which either avoid the lengthy incubation period or the danger of accidental needle sticks to health care personnel during AIDS testing.[2]

At-home testing is also a sensitive issue.[3] Medical technology companies favor such tests because the market is a lucrative one; many individuals favor such tests on the grounds that they preserve confidentiality of test results and enable those who are AIDS carriers to take earlier steps to protect themselves and others to whom they may risk transmitting the disease. Hospitals, doctors, public health officials, and many AIDS service groups oppose at-home tests because they have a relative low level of accuracy and because they do not enable the patient to receive appropriate counseling before taking the test and after learning the results.[4] One testing company attempts to balance these objectives by having a medical professional draw the blood sample for the test, and then notify the customer of the results by phone.

VALIDITY, RELIABILITY, AND COST

The EIA test for viral antibodies is relatively inexpensive—about $15. Sometimes the cost of the test itself is increased by the procedures used to transmit the results to the patient. For example, most physicians will release the results only to the patient, in person, so as to ensure confidentiality and the opportunity for counseling those who test positive.[5]

As with any test, the EIA test is not perfectly accurate. And in fact, experts disagree widely concerning its validity (accuracy). Some assert that it is very high. The routine tests of military enlistees indicated only one false positive test out of 135,000 conducted between 1985 and 1987—a false positive rate of only 0.00007%![6] Others point to data indicating a much higher rate of false positives.[7]

The Western blot test is more valid and reliable than the EIA. But it costs more ($45). It is time-consuming to conduct, and the results require interpretation.[8]

Many experts doubt that the painstaking efforts made to distinguish true positives from false positives that characterized the military testing program would be replicated in a mass screening campaign. Therefore, they generally advise against mass testing of low-risk populations because one person is likely to falsely test positive for every two properly diagnosed. The risk of false positives is therefore a distraction which might lead persons to evade testing. And the social and psychological stigma of AIDS is so great that this high a rate of false positives would not lead to effective consequences.

> If the false-positive rate is not virtually zero, screening a population in which the prevalence of HIV is low will unavoidably stigmatize and frighten many people. . . . How will these mistakes change the lives of the unfortunate individuals who are incorrectly identified as infected? . . . How many engagements should end to prevent one infection? How many jobs should be lost? How many insurance policies should be cancelled or denied? How many fetuses should be aborted, and how many couples should remain childless to avert the birth of one child with AIDS?[9]

And because of the six-month incubation period for the virus, many AIDS carriers will test as "false negatives"—they will have the virus, but not be producing antibodies to it. This means that many AIDS carriers are not identified until they succumb to opportunistic diseases that indicate the loss of immunity. At that point, tests demonstrating damage to various parts of the immune system, such as a decrease in the number of certain white blood cells (T4-lymphocytes) support the diagnosis.

These factors have led many experts to conclude that mandatory or routine screening of the general population would not do anything to slow the spread of the AIDS epidemic. Instead, it would only divert scarce public health funds from more needed detection and treatment efforts.[10] This realization has led many of those states which adopted mandatory AIDS testing for certain groups (such as applicants for marriage licenses) to repeal these laws. For example, both Louisiana and Illinois repealed their mandatory testing laws in 1988. The public health departments of both states concluded that education and counseling were a better investment of health care funds than mandatory testing of persons in low-risk groups.

However, it is possible to make a strong case for mandatory testing of high-risk populations, a case that outweighs the risk of false positives. First, AIDS tests are much more valid and reliable than drug tests. Second, the stakes are much higher with AIDS than they are with substance abuse—AIDS is a fatal, infectious disease; substance abuse is rarely fatal (in the short run) and not transmittable. Third, the health care costs for treating AIDS are greater than those for treating substance abuse, to the point that experts fear the costs of treating AIDS will bankrupt the entire health care delivery system. For reasons such as these, several states continue to test persons arrested or convicted of drug or sex offenses, and the military continues to test enlistees.[11]

SUMMARY

AIDS testing techniques are quite valid, particularly when initial AIDS antibody tests are confirmed with a Western blot test. However, the six-month incubation period for the disease means that there will be a high number of false negatives, and the relatively low incidence of the disease in the general population means that there will be some false positives. Therefore, the expense of testing and social stigma of the disease lead most experts to conclude that mass testing of low-risk groups is not an effective means of detecting AIDS or stopping its spread.

However, there are legitimate reasons to test higher risk populations, such as intravenous drug users, male homosexuals, and persons arrested for sex crimes or intravenous drug use. This is particularly true if the test results are used as the basis for educating AIDS carriers, or for more timely treatment of AIDS symptoms with medication such as AZT.

NOTES

1. Update: Serologic testing for HIV-1 antibody. (1990, June 18). *Morbidity and Mortality Weekly Report, 39*(22), pp. 380–383.

2. Edmondson, B. (1987, November). Testing the limits. *American Demographics, 8*, pp. 21–23; and Dagani, R. (1988, December 19). FDA approves five-minute AIDS test. *Chemical & Engineering News, 66*, p. 5.

3. Anderson, A. (1988, April 14). Home test kits for AIDS blocked. *Nature, 332*, p. 573; and Banned at home. (1988, April 18). *Time*, p. 26.

4. Screening programs may need to precede access to care. (1990, June 1). *AIDS Update, 3*(21), pp. 4–7; and Hardy, A., & Dawson, D. (1990, May). HIV antibody testing among adults in the United States: Data from 1988 NHIS. *American Journal of Public Health, 80*(5), pp. 586–589.

5. Kegeles, S., Catania, J., Coates, T., Pollack, L., & Lo, B. (1990). Many people who seek anonymous HIV-antibody testing would avoid it under other circumstances. *Journal of Acquired Immune Deficiency Syndromes, 4*, pp. 585–588.

6. Bishop, J. (1988, October 13). Rate of false positives from AIDS tests is very low, according to military data. *The Wall Street Journal*, p. B4.

7. Snell, J., Supran, E., Esparza, J., & Tamashiro, H. (1990, May 11). World Health Organization quality assessment programme on HIV testing. *Journal of Acquired Immune Deficiency Syndromes, 4*, pp. 803–806.

8. Hardy, A., & Dawson, D. (1990, May). HIV antibody testing among adults in the United States: Data from 1988 NHIS. *American Journal of Public Health, 80*(5), pp. 586–589.

9. Bishop, J. (1988, October 13). Rate of false positives from AIDS tests is very low, according to military data. *The Wall Street Journal*, p. B4.

10. O'Brien, M. (1989). Mandatory HIV antibody testing policies: An ethical analysis. *Bioethics, 3*(4), pp. 273–300.

11. James, F. (1989, January 9). Move to repeal Illinois AIDS law signals less strict trend in states. *The Wall Street Journal*, p. B5.

9

AIDS and the Law

AIDS is a fatal disease that has not been transmitted in the workplace except to health care workers through blood-to-blood contact. This means that AIDS raises two sets of legal issues—the rights of general employees to be provided with a safe and healthful workplace and the rights of AIDS carriers to handicap protection.

Because AIDS is such an emotionally charged issue and because it has developed so recently, the case law needed to establish legal precedents is still evolving. However, it is clear that the balance between these two sets of rights will vary depending on the nature of the position. If there is no risk of transmitting or contracting AIDS in the normal duties of the position, the rights of AIDS victims to hold positions as long as they are able to perform their duties will predominate. If there is risk of contracting AIDS in the course of the job, the right of workers to a safe and healthy workplace will predominate.[1]

OBJECTIVES

The purpose of this chapter is to:

1. Discuss the legal constraints surrounding workplace AIDS testing.

2. Discuss the liability risks employers can incur if employees are at risk of contracting AIDS from clients or co-workers.

3. Discuss the handicap discrimination laws protecting employees who are AIDS carriers (including critical differences between laws covering public and private employers).

4. Discuss how group health and life insurance carriers have responded to AIDS and how employers who offer health and/or life insurance as part of their employee benefits package are affected by these responses.

5. Discuss the liability risks employers can incur if they discriminate against employees who are AIDS carriers.

AIDS TESTING AND THE LAW

Federal and state law with respect to AIDS testing is quite new, evolving quickly, and based entirely upon federal district court rulings, state court rulings, and state human rights commission decisions.[2] These rulings embody a mixture of medical facts about the transmission of AIDS, public fears about AIDS, and legal precedents involving occupational safety and handicap rights. Generally speaking, the key issue in these cases has been whether the risk of workplace transmission was sufficient to override the otherwise paramount right of the employee to privacy against the unreasonable search and seizure represented by AIDS testing.

In *Glover v. Eastern Nebraska Community Office of Retardation*, a federal district court in Nebraska held that AIDS testing is an unconstitutional infringement upon the privacy rights of public employees. The case concerned an employee challenge to a policy requiring employees to submit to mandatory tuberculosis, hepatitis B, and AIDS testing. The policy also required employees to disclose whether they had any of the diseases. Given the minimal risk of AIDS transmission in a state hospital for the mentally retarded, the court held that the required search and seizure was unreasonable.[3]

But in another case, the U.S. District Court of Appeals for the Eastern District of Louisiana ruled (1989) that the termination of an LPN (licensed practical nurse) for refusal to submit the result of his test to determine if he was infected with the AIDS virus was not a violation of the Rehabilitation Act of 1973 or the Fourth and Fourteenth amendments. The District Court determined the termination was justified since "a hospital has a right to require such testing in order to fulfill its obligation to its employees and to the public concerning infection control and health and safety in general."[4] In addition, the court did not consider the Rehabilitation Act violated because, due to his failure to comply with the infection control policy, the employee was not otherwise qualified for employment. And finally, due to the hospital's infection control policies and the employee's relationship with an individual who had died of AIDS, he did not have a reasonable expectation of privacy with respect to his test results.[5]

While testing of applicants and employees is legal only in situations where there is risk that AIDS may be transmitted, employment discrimination in the private sector against male homosexuals in general is legal under federal law and in all states except Wisconsin.[6]

EMPLOYER LIABILITY FOR WORKPLACE TRANSMISSION OF AIDS

A relatively small percentage of employees have job duties which may involve the risk that the AIDS virus could be inadvertently transmitted to an employee through blood-to-blood contact. Examples are police officers, paramedics, and health care workers. For these occupations, two types of law make employers legally responsible for preventing conditions which encourage the spread of disease—the Occupational Safety and Health Act (OSHA), and English common law.

The OSHA, passed in 1970, created the Occupational Safety and Health Administration, responsible for developing and enforcing standards for workplace health and safety in private and public employers. The administration's enforcement authority is either direct (in that states must comply with the federal standards in an area) or indirect (in that states must adopt and enforce or to enforce standards which are at least as stringent). Twenty-five states have chosen to adopt their own occupational safety and health plans. In addition to OSHA, English common law requires that employers maintain a safe and healthy workplace for their employees.

Demonstrated violations of these laws may result in fines against the employer or in criminal charges against individual officials. In addition, both the employer and individual employees may be subject to civil suit for compensatory and/or punitive damages resulting from unsafe or unhealthy working conditions. Compensatory damages are intended to "make whole" by recompensing the employee for the costs of the illness or injury. Punitive damages are intended to punish the employer or manager for wanton, willful violations of workplace health and safety standards after the employer or its representative could reasonably be expected to know that this unsafe condition existed.

The Centers for Disease Control (CDC) report that 40 surgeons and 116 dentists and dental hygienists have been diagnosed with AIDS; the number infected with the AIDS virus is unknown but could be seven to ten times that many.[7]

Because AIDS can be spread by a variety of methods, there are real problems with conclusively proving employer liability for workplace transmission.[8] However, in the current case involving suspected infection of a dental patient by her dentist, relatively conclusive evidence for the source of the transmission has been presented. For example, molecular analysis of the DNA viral strains showed a close relationship between the DNA sequencing of the AIDS virus of the dentist and the patient. However, the qualitative criteria for determining epidemiologic linkage based on DNA sequences are just now being developed.[9] But when there is reason to assume that workplace transmission may have occurred and when the employer is at least partially negligent, a jury is likely to award civil damages to the victim (or the victim's estate if death occurs prior to the outcome of the case).

Some insurance carriers have responded to this threat by excluding AIDS from hospitals' liability coverage.[10] This means that this coverage must be purchased separately or the hospital must self-insure. But insurers are also more willing to negotiate coverage and costs because of increased self-insurance and competition in the insurance market.

However, the risk of workplace AIDS transmission and resultant liability issues appear to be non-existent in other types of jobs—there are no documented cases of transmission of AIDS in other job situations, such as schools. Despite the unfounded fears of parents, there are no risks of infection from HIV-positive teachers to children or from one child to another. Ambulance drivers, police officers, and firefighters who have assisted AIDS patients have never been infected—not even by mouth-to-mouth resuscitation.[11]

Despite the lack of documentation about the transmissibility of AIDS, there is still a high degree of public apprehension about workplace transmission. For example, a prison inmate infected with the AIDS virus recently received a 25-year sentence for trying to murder a prison guard by biting him. Despite protests that AIDS could not be transmitted through a bite, the judge concluded that the fact that the prisoner believed the disease could be so transmitted justified the severity of the sentence.[12]

HANDICAP PROTECTIONS FOR EMPLOYEES WITH AIDS

Public Agency Employers

The Rehabilitation Act of 1973 (Section 503) prevents federal government contractors and subcontractors from discriminating against qualified handicapped applicants and employees. For purposes of this law, qualified handicapped persons are those who have a physical or mental impairment which substantially limits one or more of the person's major life activities, who have a record of such impairment, or who are regarded as having such an impairment. In addition, covered agencies and contractors are required to take positive action to provide such persons with jobs by making "reasonable accommodations" which would permit the employee to perform the "primary responsibilities" of the position. Section 503 is enforced by the Department of Labor.

Section 504 of the act applies to employers that receive federal financial assistance. Unlike Section 503, it can be enforced directly in federal courts through lawsuits from individual employees or applicants who allege discrimination against them by an employer. And some federal courts have applied an exceedingly broad definition of financial assistance by finding that employers who do business with a company that receives financial assistance from the government is covered.[13]

In June 1986, the Justice Department issued an opinion stating that while AIDS was a handicap within the meaning of Section 504, employers could discriminate against employees with AIDS if it was believed, however unreasonably, that the afflicted employee was capable of transmitting the disease in the workplace. This opinion also concluded that AIDS carriers (those showing no symptoms of AIDS or ARC) were not considered handicapped under the meaning of the Rehabilitation Act of 1973.

However, this interpretation was overturned by a second opinion released in October 1988 by the Office of Legal Counsel of the Department of Justice. This opinion not only concluded that AIDS (including asymptomatic carriers) was a handicap under Section 504, but also that the unsubstantiated fear of contagion was not sufficient grounds for workplace discrimination against employees with AIDS. In reaching its decision, the department relied heavily on a prior Supreme Court decision (*School Board of Nassau County Fla. v. Arline*). In this case, the Supreme Court ruled that a school district violated Section 504 when it fired a teacher because she had chronic tuberculosis. The Court ruled that because she had not tested positive for the disease since leaving the hospital in 1978, and because her teaching performance was otherwise satisfactory, the firing had been based on society's "accumulated myths and fears" about the disease (rather than reasonable medical judgment).[14]

In a similar case involving a California school teacher, the U.S. Court of Appeals for the Ninth Circuit decided in 1988 that school officials violated the Rehabilitation Act by excluding the teacher from the classroom when medical evidence indicated that he was physically able to teach and that he would not infect his students or co-workers with AIDS through normal workplace contact.[15] Given that none of the identified cases of AIDS in the United States was known or suspected to have been transmitted from one child to another in a school, day care, or foster care setting and that a teacher infected with AIDS would not expose children to risk of infection through normal classroom contact, the school board had failed to establish reasonable medical judgment to support its contention that the teacher should have been removed from the classroom to prevent the spread of AIDS. Therefore, the court ruled that the District Court had erred in requiring that the teacher bear the burden of proving that AIDS was not contagious in a normal work setting, and in ignoring the logic established by *Arline*.

Congress codified the Supreme Court's ruling in *Arline* in legislation in 1988, as one of several amendments to Section 504 of the Rehabilitation Act of 1973.[16] That same year the U.S. Office of Personnel Management issued guidelines for federal agencies concerning AIDS in the workplace. The guidelines provide that employees who have AIDS should "be allowed to continue working so long as they are able to maintain acceptable performance and do not pose a safety or health threat to themselves or others in the workplace."[17]

AIDS is a disease that progresses quickly. Therefore, the period between an employee's showing symptoms of AIDS or ARC and being unable to perform the primary duties of the position because of the onset of full-blown AIDS is a short one, often no more than a few months or years. Public employers who might otherwise have been required to treat AIDS as a handicap have sometimes attempted to postpone a legal decision in their favor by discharging the employee because of AIDS and then requiring the employee to exhaust administrative remedies prior to a Section 504 suit in federal court. But while federal courts generally have favored the exhaustion of administrative remedies prior to a Section 504 suit, they have frowned upon this practice if the plaintiff is an AIDS victim, on the grounds that Section 504 does not specifically require the exhaustion of administrative remedies and because such delays may prevent the plaintiff from obtaining relief because of death.[18]

Private Sector Employers

Section 504 applies only to public employers. No federal legislation deals specifically with employment discrimination against AIDS carriers. But the Senate approved a bill in September 1989 that would provide punishment for employers who discriminate against persons with AIDS. And the House passed a similar bill (H.R. 2273) which was signed into law (1990) by President Bush.[19] Ironically, however, the House bill included provisions which allowed persons who come in contact with food to be assigned different duties if they have a communicable disease, including AIDS. This amendment undermines the effort of AIDS and health experts who know that the AIDS virus is not transmitted through food.[20]

Many states also have laws regulating or prohibiting AIDS testing of employees. In general, these laws extend the logic established in public agency Section 504 enforcement to private sector personnel management. That is, they define AIDS as a protected handicap, protect the confidentiality of employee medical records, and protect AIDS victims against employment discrimination.

California

In 1988, the California Supreme Court upheld a ruling by the State Fair Employment and Housing Commission that an employer violated state law when it refused to allow an employee to return to work after he had been diagnosed as having AIDS. The ruling was based on the court's conclusion that AIDS was a physical handicap under the California Employment and Housing Act, and that the employer had not proven that AIDS represented a danger to co-workers.[21]

Florida

In 1988, Florida passed legislation prohibiting employment discrimination against persons who have tested HIV positive or who have AIDS or ARC. The law also requires AIDS education for state employees, school children, university and college students, staff and clients at state-funded health agencies, correctional officers, funeral directors and embalmers, and hospital staff.

Maryland

In 1988, the Maryland Human Relations Commission ruled that HIV infection (in all stages from a positive antibody test to full-blown AIDS) is a handicap under the state's employment discrimination guidelines.[22]

Massachusetts

In 1986, a superior court held that AIDS was a protected handicap under state law. Contrary to the then- current 1986 Department of Justice ruling, the court held that employment discrimination based on a perceived fear of infection was a violation of the state handicap statute.[23]

Pennsylvania

In 1990, a Philadelphia law firm was ordered to pay $158,000 in damages, including $50,000 punitive damages, for the illegal 1987 firing of a regional partner shortly after he told his supervisor he had AIDS.[24]

Texas

A waiter with AIDS who was dismissed by his employer was awarded $60,000 in back pay and had group health insurance coverage reinstated by a jury that found he was the victim of discrimination. The restaurant had maintained that he was fired because he was sometimes late to work and had overcharged patrons. However, the jury found the restaurant guilty of violating state laws against handicap discrimination and federal laws related to an employee's right to receive insurance benefits.[25]

However, in the absence of state or local laws prohibiting or regulating AIDS testing, private sector employers may discriminate against employees with a greater degree of impunity than public agencies, for two reasons. The degree of privacy which private sector employees may reasonably expect is less extensive than for their public sector counterparts. And, under the ERISA (Employee Retirement Income Security Act) of 1974, self-funded benefit plans are not subject to state insurance laws mandating policy provisions.

Insurance Carriers

The continued spread of AIDS has led health and life insurance companies to consider use of AIDS testing to screen out high- risk applicants. Insurance companies argue that such testing is necessary to keep rates low, lest high claims from high-risk groups make up a disproportionate share of policyholders.[26] Responses to an AIDS survey conducted by the Health Insurance Association of America and the American Council of Life Insurance indicate that 91 percent of the insurers surveyed reject applicants who test positive to either AIDS antibody tests or suppressed immune systems tests.[27] The rationale behind testing is that if insurers are not allowed to screen out AIDS carriers, then other policyholders will have to sub-sidize these risks. Guidelines adopted by the National Association of Insurance Commissioners rule out considering sexual orientation in underwriting. But 30 per-cent of insurers surveyed by the Congressional Office of Technology Assessment say they do so anyway.[28]

In response to this, many public health experts and gay rights advocates have pointed out that the purpose of insurance is to assure access to quality health care, not to screen out all high-risk applicants. And besides, the cost of AIDS claims is negligible in light of total health claims. The Health Insurance Association says AIDS claims cost commerical health and life insurers only $292 million and amounted to 0.6 percent of all claims settlements in 1986, the latest year for which figures are available. But over five years through 1991, the group says health claims alone could total $10 billion.[29]

As a result of this furor, several states (among them California, the District of Columbia, and Wisconsin) have enacted legislation prohibiting insurance compa-nies from testing applicants for exposure to the AIDS virus.[30] Predictably, these laws have also drawn great opposition from insurance companies in the form of legislative lobbying to prevent prohibition of AIDS testing or threats to boycott the writing of insurance policies in a state which does not allow them to screen out high-risk applicants.[31]

It is evident that laws regulating insurance companies reflect the current uncer-tainty over the relative rights of applicants to be covered by group health policies and of insurance companies to protect themselves against preexisting conditions in members of high-risk groups. Employers suffer from this ambiguity, for they risk both lawsuits from employees if health benefits are denied or restricted, or the like-lihood of steep rate increases from health insurance carriers.

Under these circumstances, it is not surprising that many employers have elected to fund their own group health plans through self-insurance. And because ERISA (the Employee Retirement Income Security Act of 1974) exempted self-funded be-nefit plans from regulation by state insurance laws mandating policy provisions, it is quite legal for employers to develop self-funded health benefit plans that restrict coverage for AIDS.[32]

For example, one Phoenix-based national corporation decided to exclude from its self-funded health care plan coverage for illnesses that it described as "lifestyle choices," including AIDS contracted from sexual activity or intravenous drug use. It also wanted to send a message to homosexuals and drug users that they should not work for the company. But public protests forced the company to drop the pro-posed exclusion before it had the chance to consider denying a claim.[33]

And a Texas company has just adopted a lifetime medical benefit limit of $5,000 for AIDS-related treatment under its self-funded health insurance plan. This would not even cover a year's supply of AZT, much less the estimated $100,000–$250,000 lifetime medical treatment cost for AIDS. But an employee of this com-pany diagnosed as having AIDS is suing his employer and the employer's former health insurer that now administers the self-funded plan for the full $1 million of coverage he would have been entitled to under the previous plan.[34]

Insurance experts point out that employer attempts to limit health plan sublimit coverage for items such as pregnancy have only invited increased regulation by Congress and state legislatures. They fear that opening up the issue of eliminating sublimits on AIDS-related coverage would explode into a debate on amending ERISA to mandate the entire scope of self-funded group health plans, down to required limits, deductibles, and even employer contributions. And that sort of regulation would not be in the interest of self-funded health plans, the agencies that administer them, or the employers that fund them.[35]

EMPLOYER LIABILITY FOR DISCRIMINATING AGAINST EMPLOYEES WITH AIDS

Shuttleworth also addressed the question of appropriate damages in a Section 504 action. The court ordered the county to rehire the employee with back pay and attorneys' fees, to reinstate his health and life insurance benefits, and to pay his back medical bills which would have been reimbursed had he remained on the payroll.

SUMMARY

AIDS is a fatal disease that is very difficult to transmit in the workplace—except for health care jobs. Since there is no known risk of transmitting or contracting AIDS in the normal duties of non-health-care positions, the rights of AIDS victims to hold these positions as long as they are able to perform the duties of the position will outweigh the fears of other employees about contracting AIDS from co-workers. This is especially true for government agencies or contractors because of Section 504 handicap protections, but many states have laws which also prevent similar discrimination against handicapped persons by private employers. Employers who violate these laws are subject to compensatory and punitive damages.

Group health and life insurance carriers are facing the threat of AIDS by seeking to exclude those who test positive for the AIDS virus or to limit payouts for AIDS for those covered by the policy. While present laws allow the exemption of self-insured benefit plans from ERISA, use of these plans by employers to evade or limit coverage for AIDS is likely to invite increased regulation of self-insured plans through ERISA amendments at the federal level or through similar state laws.

NOTES

1. Cohen, C., & Cohen, M. (1989, July). AIDS in the workplace: Legal requirements and organizational responses. *Labor Law Journal, 40*, pp. 411–418.

2. Gostin, L. (1990, April 18). The AIDS litigation project: A national review of court and human rights commission decisions, part II: Discrimination. *Journal of the American Medical Association, 263*(15), pp. 2086–2093.

3. Glover v. Eastern Nebraska Community Office of Retardation, No, 87-0-830 (D. Neb. March 29, 1988).

4. Kevin Leckelt v. Board of Commissioners of Hospital District No. 1, Docket 86-4235, March 15, 1989.

5. Reichenberg, N. (1989, June). Legal issues in the public sector: Termination for failure to submit AIDS test results upheld. *IPMA News*. Alexandria, VA: International Personnel Management Association, p. 7.

6. Schachter, V., Geidt, T., & von Seeburg, S. (1987, September). Legal AIDS: An enlightened corporate policy. *Across the Board, 24*(9), pp. 48–53.

7. Staver, S. (1990, September 7). Infected staff may face more restrictions. *American Medical News*, p. 3.

8. Staver, S. (1990, September 7). Stumbling blocks keep questions in dental HIV case. *American Medical News*, p. 26.

9. Possible transmission of human immunodeficiency virus to a patient during an invasive dental procedure. (1990, July 27). *Morbidity and Mortality Weekly Report, 39*(29), pp. 489–493.

10. Changing times restrict insurance coverage. (1989, May 20). *Hospitals*, p. 82.

11. The facts about AIDS: A special NEA higher education advocate report. (1988). *NEA Higher Education Advocate*. Washington, D.C.: National Education Association, p. 6.

12. Sullivan, J. (1990, May 19). 25 year sentence for biting guard. *The New York Times*, p. 10.

13. Frazier v. Board of Trustees of Northwest Mississippi Regional Medical Center, 765 F. 2nd 1278 (5th Cir. 1985).

14. 107 S. Ct 1123 (1987).

15. Chalk v. United States District Court, Central District of California, 840 F. 2nd (9th Cir. 1988).

16. Civil rights bill becomes law. (1988, May). *IPMA News*. Alexandria, VA: International Personnel Management Association, p. 5

17. AIDS guidelines released. (1988, May). *IPMA News*. Alexandria, VA: International Personnel Management Association, pp. 1, 8.

18. Shuttleworth v. Broward County, 639 F. Supp (S.D. Fla. 1986).

19. Fletcher, M. (1990, April 16). Hyatt legal services told to pay damages for firing AIDS victim. *Business Insurance*, pp. 3, 15.

20. King, G. (1990, June 2). [Letter to the editor]. Pandering to ignorance on AIDS. *The New York Times*, p. 18.

21. Raytheon Co. v. Fair Employment and Housing Commission (Cal. S. Ct. April 22, 1988).

22. Maryland rights agency adds HIV infection to definition. (1988). *77 Daily Labor Report*. Washington, D.C.: BNA, A-12.

23. Cronin v. New England Telephone, 1 Individual Employee Rights Cases (BNA) 651 (Mass. Super. Ct. 1986).

24. Fletcher, M. (1990, April 16). Hyatt legal services told to pay damages for firing AIDS victim. *Business Insurance*, pp. 3, 15.

25. Waiter with AIDS wins $60,000 in a job bias case. (1990, May 19). *The New York Times*, p. 10.

26. Melloan, G. (1988, May 31). Insurers try to cope with AIDS test barriers. *The Wall Street Journal*, p. 25.

27. Myers, P. (1987, January). Pooling the AIDS risk. *Best's Review, Life/Health Edition*, pp. 38–40, 120.

28. Ricklefs, R. (1988, April 26). Gay-rights groups and insurers battle over required AIDS tests. *The Wall Street Journal, p. 41.*

29. Ibid.

30. Kohout, M. (1987, July 15). States ban insurers' AIDS tests. *Public Administration Times*, pp. 1, 7.

31. Dederer, J. (1987, January). The AIDS testing predicament. *Best's Review, Life/ Health Edition*, pp. 38–39.

32. Opinions: Protect AIDS patients. (1989, December 4). *Business Insurance*, p. 8.

33. Ibid.

34. Ibid.

35. Ibid.

10

AIDS Policies and Practices

AIDS is an increasingly serious public health problem in this country. Its seriousness has led the public to respond with denial and then panic. Ironically, both these responses have prevented us from addressing AIDS as a public policy issue and from developing coherent strategies for containment and treatment of this disease.

AIDS is a critical workplace issue for three reasons. First, it requires employers to develop policies for protecting the rights of employees with AIDS, just as they would victims of other progressive disabilities. Second, it requires employers to develop health benefit programs which balance the need for AIDS coverage with the costs of such coverage. Third, employers must develop educational programs to reduce employees' irrational fear of catching AIDS in the workplace.

Health care employers have a different set of priorities. First, they must develop infection control policies which recognize that AIDS can be transmitted in the workplace and prevent clients or employees with AIDS from transmitting the disease. Second, they must develop health benefit and risk management (liability) programs which balance the need for AIDS coverage with the costs of such coverage. Third, they must develop educational programs to train employees how to eliminate the risk of catching AIDS in the workplace while continuing to provide compassionate and professional health care to patients who have the disease.

OBJECTIVES

The purpose of this chapter is to:

1. Describe the AIDS policies now used by major public and private employers in the United States, emphasizing emergent policies and practices where most employers do not yet have them.

2. Discuss how an effective AIDS education and training program can help counteract employees' irrational fears about catching AIDS in the workplace.

3. Show how an EAP (employee assistance program) can help employees who are AIDS victims deal with the realities of AIDS.

4. Present some effective strategies now used by major public and private employers to limit health care costs and personal liability, while at the same time providing meaningful AIDS coverage for employees.

5. Specify the personnel policies and practices which health care employers must adopt to prevent the workplace transmission of AIDS, recognize the rights of employees, and provide professional and compassionate health care to AIDS-infected patients.

WORKPLACE AIDS POLICIES AND PRACTICES

Experts on AIDS in the workplace estimate that fewer than 10 percent of employers in the United States have developed policies in this area.[1] Given the potential dangers of AIDS with respect to health care costs and legal liability, and employees' irrational fear of catching AIDS in the workplace, this lack of policy development is troubling. It means that employers need to move beyond their own denial and panic to develop clear guidelines which address their employees' fears while meeting the employers' objectives—productivity, health care cost containment, and legal liability risk management.

It should be clear at this point that workplace AIDS policy is not nearly as developed as is workplace substance abuse policy. Therefore, the policy guidelines presented below are not merely a compilation of the current policies of employers. They are also recommendations which employers may wish to consider when framing their own AIDS policies and practices. They are intended to help employers meet their objectives while maintaining an awareness of the progress of the disease in society and legal constraints related to employee rights.

Bear in mind that these are recommendations for general employers. They may be augmented or contradicted by recommendations for health care employers, which follow, because of their differing needs and characteristics.

AIDS Testing as a Selection or Promotion Criterion

Applicants should not be tested for AIDS as a condition of employment. Legally, both public and private employers risk lawsuits if they use blood testing as a condition of employment, unless they can show that the test is related to ability to do the job. Since most persons who test positive for AIDS are asymptomatic, it would not be possible for an employer to legally reject them for employment if they were otherwise qualified for the position. It is always possible for personnel directors to claim another reason for rejection (such as inadequate education or experience for the position), but this reason will be subject to the same types of tests as are applied to employers who systematically reject minority, female, or handicapped applicants. That is, a pattern of discrimination which results in the exclusion of all persons who test positive for the AIDS virus makes it impossible for the employer to defend the validity of selection or promotion decisions.

Employers may legitimately reject applications from persons who show signs of ARC, provided that they can document that these symptoms would prevent the applicant from performing the required duties of the position. It is important to remember here that the handicap protections of "reasonable accommodation" apply only to current employees, not applicants. The employer is not required to make accommodation of any kind to applicants, only to show whether in fact they can satisfactorily perform the required duties of the position as it is defined.

How Do You Find Out if an Employee Has AIDS?

Employers will generally find out that an employee has AIDS either voluntarily or involuntarily. If the former, the employee will inform the supervisor that the employee has AIDS. Voluntary disclosure is quite risky for the employee because it may expose the employee to disciplinary action, undesirable job modification, or loss of medical confidentiality if the medical condition is made public.

For the employee, the purpose of voluntary disclosure is to advise the employer that it may be necessary for the employer to undertake reasonable job modifications so that the employee may continue to hold a job. The employee will almost always want to continue working. Work is a source of social contacts, professional stature, and personal satisfaction. It is also the cheapest avenue for acquiring group health and life insurance, which the AIDS victim urgently needs to pay for current or anticipated expenses.

The employer may suspect that an employee has AIDS if the employee begins to show obvious physical signs of ARC such as rapid weight loss. Or the employee may show increased absenteeism or tardiness due to the onset of opportunistic infections. Or co-workers may spread rumors that an employee has AIDS.

Since medical information is confidential unless the employee chooses to disclose it, the employer can do nothing to assist the employee who does not voluntarily advise that he or she has AIDS. However, the employer should continue to handle performance problems through the normal process of informal and formal counseling, focusing on the employee's behavior rather than seeking to induce the employee to involuntarily disclose his or her medical condition.

Reasonable Accommodation

An employee with AIDS is entitled to retain his or her job as long as the employer can make reasonable accommodations that allow him or her to perform the primary duties of the position satisfactorily. This means that a job analysis should be completed to identify the critical elements of the job, reasonable performance standards, and physical skills and abilities needed for their performance.

If the employee carries the AIDS virus but is asymptomatic, no job motifications will be necessary. If the employee shows some symptoms of ARC, minor modifications may be necessary to reduce the amount of physical exertion the job requires. For example, the employee and the supervisor should look at jobs which require standing, walking, climbing stairs, etc., to see if duties can be modified to make them less arduous.

If the essential tasks of the position are strenuous, it may be necessary to move the employee to a "light-duty" position, if any are available. The objective here is to enable the employee to remain on the payroll as long as possible, rather than move quickly to a leave without pay or disability retirement status. If there are no light-duty positions available, or if the employee's condition has progressed so far that he or she is unable to perform even light duties, then the employee remains on the payroll until sick leave, vacation, and all other forms of leave are exhausted.

Because AIDS strikes relatively young employees, few will have enough years of service to qualify for a disability retirement. However, they should be given all the disability benefits and continued health and life insurance coverage to which they are entitled under the employer's personnel policies or collective bargaining agreement. In particular, their health and life insurance coverage should be continued after they are separated from the payroll. Under COBRA (Comprehensive Omnibus Budget Reconciliation Act) regulations, employers are required to make health insurance available to employees for eighteen months following separation, for cost plus a 1 percent fee for administrative expenses. But many employees do not know this and do not ask that their employers make this available to them.

Employees who are AIDS victims should receive detailed counseling concerning their handicap rights, disability retirement, health benefits, and life insurance. The counseling should be provided either by the personnel department or the EAP. The counseling should recognize that employees with AIDS seek to remain on the payroll as long as possible and to receive insurance benefits as long as possible following separation.

COMBATTING EMPLOYEE FEARS THROUGH AN EFFECTIVE AIDS EDUCATION PROGRAM

Devastating as are the effects of AIDS for its victims, they are also traumatic for co-workers. The number of employees with AIDS in most organizations will be relatively low—probably no more than 0.5 percent or 1.0 percent. This is much less than the number who will die from heart attacks, cancer, or automobile accidents. But AIDS has a more serious impact on employees because it strikes at so many of our fears. It is almost entirely preventable, it is fatal, and it is transmitted primarily through homosexual practices and IV drug use.

What are some possible results of hysterical employee reactions to AIDS? Co-workers may shun employees who are suspected of having AIDS—or they may harass these employees in an effort to make them quit their jobs. Unions may threaten to strike unless the identity of AIDS victims is divulged and the victims are fired. Or the employer's bill for plumbing repairs will rise as employees clean toilet seats with paper towels to prevent catching AIDS from an infected co-worker.

All of these reactions leave the employer subject to lawsuit because they are violations of the employee's right to privacy and confidentiality of medical records. They also violate the employee's handicap rights if they lead to employment discrimination against an AIDS victim who is asymptomatic or otherwise able to perform job duties successfully. And once employees react, it will be difficult for management to respond in a way which both respects the rights of AIDS victims and speaks clearly and directly to the fears of co-workers.

Start the Education Program Immediately

The best way to avoid panic reactions by employees is for the employer to immediately initiate an AIDS education program for all employees.[2] This program should be mandatory for all supervisors and employees. It should emphasize the following points:[3]

1. *AIDS is not transmittable in the workplace*. Use the material presented in Chapter 7 or any of the source material provided there to tell employees that AIDS cannot be transmitted or contracted except through blood-to-blood contact with an infected individual. Nor can it be transmitted through any other means except sexual relations, intravenous drug use, a transfusion from infected blood, or between mother and child during pregnancy and nursing.

2. *AIDS victims are legally entitled to handicap protection*. Use the material presented in Chapter 9 or other source materials to define the handicap protections to which employees with AIDS are entitled. Emphasize that AIDS is considered a handicap, and that employees with AIDS are entitled to retain their jobs, provided they can with reasonable accommodation perform them satisfactorily. Remind employees that AIDS victims are entitled to "light-duty" positions, if any are available, as an alternative to being removed from the workplace once their leave is exhausted. Explain that it is illegal to discriminate against employees on the basis of their being AIDS carriers. Emphasize that harassment of AIDS victims by co-workers or supervisors is not only illegal, but subjects the employer to punitive damages for allowing discrimination against handicapped persons. Tell employees and supervisors that they will be disciplined if they harass co-workers who have AIDS.

3. *The employer provides many economic benefits to AIDS victims and their sur-vivors.* Summarize the elements of your benefits policies and programs which may be used to assist employees with AIDS or their survivors. Include light-duty posi-tions, disability retirement, and health and life insurance benefits for employees. Add information on employer-financed health and life insurance benefits which may extend beyond the period of active employment. Lastly, explain the retirement, life insurance and Social Security benefits to which survivors of the employee are entitled after the employee dies.

4. *Medical records are confidential.* AIDS is a medical condition which (at least initially) does not affect most victims' ability to perform their jobs. Therefore, it should be treated confidentially. The only two people who need to know are the immediate supervisor and one person in the personnel department (so that reason-able accommodation or other strategies to help keep the victim employable may occur). Other release of the information (such as to co-workers or union officials) is a violation of the employee's right to privacy and subjects the employer to puni-tive damages in a lawsuit brought by the employee.

5. *Voluntary disclosure enables AIDS victims to get better treatment and hold their jobs longer.* Employees who have AIDS may be hesitant to reveal this to their supervisor because they fear that they will be ostracized, fired, or otherwise dis-criminated against. Make sure employees understand that the employer will prevent these things from happening, insofar as it is humanly possible to do so. Use current information to emphasize that prompt detection and treatment of AIDS can extend the life of the victim, perhaps indefinitely. This means the AIDS victim can have the disease and still function well longer at work. And the AIDS victim can enjoy life longer and better provide for survivors even if the disease progresses to ARC or full-blown AIDS.

6. *Employees will not be subject to mandatory AIDS testing.* AIDS is not trans-mittable in the workplace. Even if it were, the technology of AIDS testing is not accurate. The six-month incubation period of the virus guarantees that many per-sons who can transmit the disease will still test negative for AIDS virus antibodies. And some people who do not have the disease will falsely test positive. This means that workplace AIDS testing of applicants or employees is not a cost-efficient or effective means of detecting AIDS carriers or stopping the spread of the disease.

7. *AIDS victims deserve compassion, not punishment.* Remind employees that AIDS is a disease caused by a virus. The disease is painful, debilitating, and fatal. While it may be transmitted by practices resulting from lifestyle choices (anal in-tercourse by male homosexuals or needle sharing by intravenous drug users), it has also been transmitted accidentally. And many victims, such as newborn infants, surely have had no choice in whether they were born with the AIDS virus. Conse-quently, work to get employees to realize that blaming the victims is often a defen-sive reaction caused by other employees' own irrational fear of catching AIDS in the workplace.

8. *The employer's AIDS policies and procedures will be public information.* Pa-tients, employees, health and life insurance carriers, and outside accrediting bodies

will be advised of the workplace AIDS policies and procedures that the employer has adopted.

AN EAP CAN HELP EMPLOYEES WHO ARE AIDS VICTIMS

If the employer has an EAP with a broadly defined role which includes counseling and referral for a range of personal issues that affect employee productivity, the EAP's responsibilities should include counseling and referral services for employees who have AIDS and for their immediate family members. It will be the function of the EAP to clarify employer policies to employees who have AIDS or fear they may have it. Counseling may include such topics as handicap protection, reasonable accommodation, available benefits, and confidentiality of medical records. If necessary, the EAP will refer the employee to counseling and support groups in the community (see Appendix C), or to health care providers for appropriate services covered under the employer's health benefits policy.

Counseling and referral services will be kept strictly confidential. If the employee who has AIDS does not wish to divulge this to his or her supervisor, the EAP will respect the employee's privacy. It will then be up to the supervisor to initiate disciplinary action if and when the employee can no longer perform the duties of the position without reasonable accommodation.

If the EAP has a more narrowly defined role (alcohol abuse treatment), the personnel department should also offer AIDS counseling and referral services directly to employees and family members.

LIMITING HEALTH CARE COSTS

Employers must recognize that health insurance carriers have had much the same reaction to AIDS as employees. That is, the threat of incurring a major payout of unknown proportions has caused them to react with defensiveness and panic. Therefore, the best strategy employers can adopt is to deal rationally with insurance companies to make sure that the costs of AIDS coverage for employees are reasonably related to the risks assumed by the insurance companies. If it is not possible to obtain adequate coverage at a reasonable cost, the employer may wish to consider options: self-funding, employee funding, reduced sub-benefit coverage, or increased reliance on contractual or leased employee services.

Make Sure Benefit Costs Are Reasonably Related to Risks

Like employees and employers, health insurance carriers' first reaction to AIDS is likely to be panic. After all, it is a fatal disease that strikes young employees during their productive work years, costing $100,000–$250,000 from onset to death. Even if the incidence of the AIDS virus among employees is less than 1 percent, and even if only 30 percent of those carrying the virus will later develop ARC or full-blown AIDS, they are still likely to panic at first. This is because they are uncertain how to screen out high-risk applicants or to price health benefits coverage so that payment of AIDS benefits does not draw down the fund.

Employers can anticipate this reaction by negotiating sensibly with insurance carriers over AIDS coverage costs. Employers should use the insurance industry's own figures (presented in this chapter and Chapter 7) to argue that the total cost of life and health insurance benefits for AIDS victims is neither high (in comparison with total payouts) nor unpredictable. Employers should remember that while the insurance industry in general is panicked by AIDS, it is also a competitive industry—carriers are willing to negotiate coverage and rates if they estimate that the policy is profitable or they consider the employer a valuable client.

Trade a Longer Waiting Period for Lower Benefit Costs

The major problem with predicting the incidence of AIDS in a given work force is that applicants and employees may carry the AIDS virus for a relatively long incubation period before producing antibodies or showing symptoms of AIDS. And it cannot be denied that access to affordable group health and life insurance is a major reason people decide to enter the work force, or to change jobs to a major public or private employer.

Under these circumstances, the employer may be able to negotiate a lower health or life insurance benefit rate by excluding not only preexisting conditions from coverage but by excluding AIDS-related conditions which appear during the first year of employment. This one-year waiting period applies only to employees who test positive for AIDS, show positive symptoms of ARC, or develop AIDS during the first year of employment. One health insurance carrier, Golden Rule Insurance Company of Indianapolis, already offers such coverage to employers.

If this one-year waiting period coincides with the probationary period for new employees, employers should be extremely wary of pressures to use an unsatisfactory performance evaluation at the end of the probationary period as an underhanded means of discharging employees whose performance is satisfactory but who are suspected of having AIDS. Once a one-year waiting period is established, the employer must base retention decisions solely on performance and let the insurance carrier contest claims if it thinks they are submitted in violation of the waiting period. To act otherwise is to risk civil and criminal liability for violation of employment rights for handicapped persons, even if this collusion with the insurance carrier results in some short-term financial savings in the cost of coverage.

Self-Funded Benefit Plans

If reasonable health insurance coverage for AIDS or ARC is simply not available, the employer may wish to avoid the cost of health insurance premiums altogether and simply put them into a fund to cover claims directly. This option (self-insurance) has already become increasingly attractive to large employers because it may be much cheaper than purchasing an insurance policy. This means that any health or life insurance savings caused by an EAP, wellness program, or QWL (quality of work life program) are retained directly by the employer. It makes the employer much more accountable for risk management. If there are a large enough number of employees to make the risks predictable and the fund large enough to survive payouts for one or two severe illnesses, the employer may wish to self-insure alone. If the employer is smaller, it is also possible to join a self-insured association managed by risk-management consultants.

One attractive feature of self-funded benefit plans is that they are exempt from regulation by the federal government or state governments under ERISA (Employee Retirement Income Security Act of 1974). This means than an individual employer or an association can establish a self-funded health benefit plan that is tailored to the objectives of the employer or the types of health care costs it wishes to assume. For example, a self-funded plan can exclude or limit coverage for the costs of illness or death caused by so-called "lifestyle choices." For example, it can exclude claims by smokers for illnesses related to smoking, for drug or alcohol treatment programs, or for AIDS.

While the ability to tailor a benefit program to reduce risks and influence employees' health habits may seem attractive to employers, two cautionary notes are in order. First, employees' motivation and productivity may be negatively influenced by attempts to invade their private lives by manipulating benefit coverage— particularly if the employer cannot demonstrate a reasonable relationship between productivity and the items excluded from coverage. Given that employees infected with the AIDS virus show no symptoms initially (if ever), it would seem impossible to demonstrate a link between AIDS and productivity. Second, given the increasing popularity of self-funding as a health benefits coverage strategy, wholesale meddling by self-funded insurance plan administrators will only increase pressure from unions and public health interest groups on Congress and state legislatures to regulate this type of plan. The end result will be closer management of these plans to prevent exclusions based on lifestyle choices, on the grounds that these exclusions are an unreasonable invasion of privacy or merely an effort by employers to pass legitimate business costs onto a public health system that is already stretched far beyond its ability to pay.[4] Thus, sub-benefit limitations for AIDS or ARC should be adopted cautiously, if at all, due to the probability of an unfavorable reaction from employees, public opinion, or political leaders. The short-term savings may not be worth the long-term price. And third, embarking on a self-funded benefit plan without a large enough fund to cover payouts, or a stop-loss provision on each case, can result in bankruptcy for the small employer.[5]

Employee-Funded Benefit Plans

Employers who are unable to purchase meaningful coverage at reasonable rates and who are unable or unwilling to self-insure may bring employees into the picture by asking them to either assume an increasing share of the costs or select lower benefits in the form of greater exclusions, deductibles, or other expenses. While this option is likely to be unpopular with employees, it may be considerably more popular than the remaining alternative, which is to carry no group health or life insurance at all. Employers should remember that ERISA does not require private employers to carry pension or health benefit coverage for their employees. It only requires those employers who elect to do so to meet certain minimum standards for the stability and security of pension, health benefit, and life insurance funds.

However, state law may require employers to carry health benefits coverage if they have more than a specified number of employees. This is the case in Massachusetts and other states.

Increased Reliance on Contractual or Leased Employee Services

The ultimate employer strategy for reducing health and life insurance costs is to deliberately reduce legal and financial liability by systematically increasing the percentage of employees who receive no health or life insurance benefits—part-time employees, temporary employees, reemployed annuitants, leased employees, or those hired under contractual service agreements.

This means that the employer will in effect adopt an implicit two-tier personnel system similar to the model described in the Introduction. First-tier employees, primarily managerial and professional, will receive a benefits package along with their salary. If there is a strong union presence, unionized employees will also be included in this first-tier personnel system as a result of the benefit provisions comprising their collective bargaining agreement. Increasingly, all other employees will be hired on an as-needed basis, without benefits. They will be hired directly, or indirectly through a contractor or leasing agent.

The big advantage that two-tier personnel systems offer the employer is a chance to reduce benefit costs. Employees with low salaries usually receive the same health and life insurance benefits as managers and executives earning many times their salaries. The result is a benefits system that may cost an average of 45 percent of direct salary costs, less that this percentage for professional and managerial employees, more than this percentage for other employees. Wouldn't it be cheaper and more efficient, given workload fluctuations, to reduce benefit costs and eliminate superfluous employees by relying increasingly on second-tier employment strategies?

And because second-tier employees are hired on an as-needed basis, they are never eligible for permanent status at the end of a probationary period. They may be let go at will, without cause, and without due process. They may be discharged because they have AIDS, or merely because someone thinks they may have AIDS. But because the employer can always claim that they were discharged simply because there was no further need for their services, it would be extremely difficult for employees to document a persuasive case demonstrating that they were discharged in violation of federal or state laws prohibiting handicap discrimination in the workplace.

Of course, there are many serious negative implications of two-tier personnel systems—invidious racial or gender discrimination, economic and social instability, and the externalization of health costs for these employees to society as a whole. These negative implications will be discussed in the Conclusion. But in the short run, they represent a cost savings and a reduction of liability risks to the employer, while enabling the employer to externalize risks of both AIDS and substance abuse to society as a whole. This is particularly true if the employer can convince managerial and professional employees that their own job security, organizational stature, and relative affluence depend upon the existence of a larger group of marginalized clerical employees and laborers who are treated as commodities to be exploited and then discarded when they are no longer needed.

INFECTION CONTROL AND RISK MANAGEMENT POLICIES FOR HEALTH CARE EMPLOYERS

Health care facilities (hospitals, doctors, dentists, and nursing homes) are a special category of employer because there is some risk that AIDS can be transmitted from clients to employees, or from employees to clients, in the course of normal job duties.[6] This transmission is most likely to occur during invasive surgical procedures when blood from a patient mixes with blood from a surgeon or nurse due to an accidental cut, needle stick, or skin opening. Health care workers who have primary responsibility for intravenous procedures, renal dialysis, and the drawing of blood samples are also at significantly higher risk.

The Centers for Disease Control report that at least 27 health care workers worldwide are believed to have become infected with AIDS from job-related exposure, and another 66 might possibly fall into this category.[7] In addition, there is at least one case where a dental patient may have been infected by an AIDS-positive dentist during invasive oral surgery.[8]

The risk of AIDS transmission from a single needle stick is slight—about 0.4 percent, the same as from an individual instance of unprotected anal intercourse with an AIDS-positive man. Yet the fear of AIDS is so strong that health care workers routinely assume that the CDC underestimates the risk of workplace infection and take their own precautions.[9] For example, surgeons who operate on AIDS-positive patients sometimes use waterproof boots, waterproof aprons, face shields, double gloves, and double sleeves. And all hospitals have adopted "universal precautions," infection control procedures which are designed to prevent accidental blood contact.

In practice, however, it is not possible to eliminate the risk of AIDS transmission without negatively affecting patient care. Many emergency room doctors, nurses, and paramedics routinely risk this contact in order to save a patient's life. They must undertake invasive surgical procedures without knowing whether a patient is AIDS-positive and without the time to protect themselves adequately against blood contact. In addition, some of the precautions taken to minimize the risk of AIDS transmission can also contribute to the dehumanization of care and the isolation of AIDS patients.

But the personal, legal, and financial risks which AIDS imposes on individuals and employers requires that these challenges be faced. It requires that each health care employer develop an infection control policy which minimizes the possibility of workplace infection and protects the employment rights of AIDS victims insofar as possible. The primary elements of such a policy are presented below and described in detail when they differ significantly from those presented previously as applicable to employers in general:

1. *No employees will be tested for AIDS.* And even if there were a risk, AIDS testing is neither an efficient nor an effective means of detecting AIDS carriers or preventing the spread of the disease. While patients and employees may fear this risk and hospitals may wish to respond to this fear under the threat of losing patients,[10] under *Arline* this fear is not a justifiable reason for violating the privacy of employees or restricting their right to hold jobs in the health care field.

2. *All employees are required to learn and comply with infection control procedures which prevent the transmission of AIDS through needle sticks or other accidents.* All new and current employees will be required to sign a statement attesting that they understand these policies and procedures and will comply with them. Employees will not be allowed to engage in duties which involve the risk of transmission until this training is completed. Employees who do not complete the training or do not comply with policies and procedures while on the job, will be subject to disciplinary action, including termination.

Like most issues involving organizational ethics, this issue emphasizes the underlying conflict between employee protection and organizational efficiency. Obviously, employees who always observe maximum infection control procedures will spend so much time washing, gloving, and donning protective garments and goggles that they will be able to give only a minimum level of patient care. And employees who ignore these procedures entirely will subject themselves and the hospital to the risk of contracting AIDS through accidental needle sticks or other unsafe practices. So health care employers must communicate two messages to employees: infection control procedures are necessary, but don't go overboard if you want to get your work done. In making choices as to how strict they will be in following infection control procedures, employees must be informed concerning which patients have AIDS and must use their own judgment to determine the appropriate balance between efficiency and protection.

3. *Employees who feel they may have been exposed to AIDS on the job are required to report the incident immediately. If they so request, these employees will be tested for AIDS. If they test positive, they will be removed from positions involving the risk of blood-to-blood contact with patients or other employees.*

The dilemma here is that health care facilities must be able to document possible cases of AIDS exposure through an incident reporting system. This is necessary to resolve liability and wrokers compensation cases. And once the employer knows that an employee has tested positive for AIDS, that employee cannot be allowed to perform job duties which involve the risk of infecting patients or other employees. On the other hand, it is necessary to maintain employee privacy by avoiding random or universal testing of employees. In this situation, it is quite possible that health care workers who know they have AIDS will hide this information from their employer for fear of losing their jobs. And employers will acquiesce because they do not want to test employees unless they are forced to do so. But employees who choose this course of action must recognize that they are not entitled to handicap protections, and an employer may get rid of them for other reasons if the employer suspects that they may have AIDS.

4. *Employees who are AIDS victims are entitled to the same handicap protections as are employees outside the health care field.*

5. *Employee medical records are confidential.*

6. *The employer will provide AIDS education and referral services for all employees.* The educational program will include information about how AIDS is transmitted. It will emphasize the handicap protections to which AIDS victims are legally entitled, the confidentiality of their medical records, the health and life insurance benefits the employer provides to them and their survivors, and the fact that early identification of employees who are AIDS victims enables them to get better treatment and live longer.

The employer will provide AIDS counseling and referral services through the EAP to employees who have AIDS or to members of their immediate family. These services will be completely confidential, unless continued confidentiality would violate the employer's infection control policy or unless the disease has progressed to the point that the employee is unable to perform the duties of the position without reasonable accommodation by the employer. In these instances, the employee's immediate supervisor and the personnel director will be the only persons notified (because they need to know).

7. *The employer's AIDS policies and procedures will be public information.* Patients, employees, health and life insurance carriers, and outside accrediting bodies will be advised of the employer's workplace AIDS policies and procedures.

8. *AIDS victims deserve compassion, not punishment.* Remind employees that AIDS is a disease caused by a virus. The disease is painful, debilitating, and fatal. While it may be transmitted by practices resulting from lifestyle choices (anal intercourse by male homosexuals or needle sharing by intravenous drug users), it has also been transmitted accidentally. And many victims, such as newborn infants, surely have had no choice in whether they were born with the AIDS virus. Consequently, work to get employees to realize that blaming the victims is often a defensive reaction caused by other employees' own irrational fear of catching AIDS in the workplace.

SUMMARY

AIDS is not yet a significant problem for most employers. But employees' panicky reactions to it, and the unforseeable health care costs and liability risks it poses for the future, require that employers anticipate these reactions by immediately adopting workplace AIDS policies and procedures. Most important among these is an employee education program which can counteract employee fears by emphasizing that AIDS is not transmittable in the workplace and that AIDS victims are entitled to compassion and to legal protection against employment discrimination or harassment. The EAP can play an important role in AIDS counseling and referral services.

Health care employers must recognize that AIDS cannot be transmitted from employees to patients or other employees through legitimate workplace activity. Therefore, neither employees nor applicants should be tested for AIDS. Because there is a slight possibility that AIDS can be transmitted from patients to employees through accidental needle sticks, health care employers should adopt infection control policies and teach them in orientation and training programs, so that this risk is minimized.

Employers should investigate a number of available strategies for providing employees with meaningful health and life insurance benefits at reasonable cost. Or they may wish to join the increasing trend toward externalizing the cost of AIDS treatment or the risk of handicap discrimination completely by utilizing a secondary employment market (temporary, part-time employees hired "at will" without benefits) whenever possible.

NOTES

1. Masi, D. (1987, July). AIDS in the workplace: What can be done? *Personnel, 64*, pp. 57–60.

2. Emery, A. (1989, June). AIDS strategies that work. *Business and Health*, pp. 43–46; Westbrook, L. (1988, July). The corporate community ponders AIDS. *Business and Health*, pp. 8–9; and Schachter, V., Geidt, T., & von Seeburg, S. (1987, September). Legal AIDS: An enlightened corporate policy. *Across the board, 24*(9), pp. 48–53.

3. Lutgen, L. (1987, November). AIDS in the workplace: Fighting fear with facts and policy. *Personnel, 64*, pp. 53–57; and Jenks, J. (1987, September). Protecting privacy rights. *Personnel Journal, 66*, pp. 123–126.

4. Haggerty, A. (1987, June 22). Aetna denies charge by gay rights group. *National Underwriter Life & Health—Financial Services Edition*, p. 61; and Faden, R., & Kass, N. (1988, April). Health insurance and AIDS: The issue of state regulatory activity. *The American Journal of Public Health, 78*, pp. 437–438.

5. Faden, R., & Kass, N. (1988, April). Health insurance and AIDS: The issue of state regulatory activity. *The American Journal of Public Health, 78*, pp. 437–438.

6. Moskop, J. (1990, Summer). AIDS and hospitals: The policy options. *Health Services Administration, 35*(2), pp. 159–171.

7. Health care workers. (1990, June). *AIDS Report, 3*(11), pp. 5–6.

8. Possible transmission of human immunodeficiency virus to a patient during an invasive dental procedure. (1990, July 27). *Morbidity and Mortality Weekly Report, 39*(29), pp. 489–493.

9. Rosenthal, E. (1990, November 11). Practice of medicine is changing under specter of the AIDS virus. *The New York Times*, pp. 1, 17.

10. Burda, D. (1988, March 24). Hospital's employee AIDS testing upheld. *Modern Healthcare*, *19*, p. 4; Smith, S. (1989, May 13). AIDS test polarizes debate on surgery, safety, and privacy. *New Scientist*, *122*, p. 31.

11

Conclusion: Workplace Drug and AIDS Policies Are a Metaphor for Our Future

SUBSTANCE ABUSE AND AIDS ARE RELATED

Substance abuse and AIDS are interrelated issues which are testing the ability of human resource managers to develop solutions which are technically feasible compromises between two important values: efficiency and employee rights. These issues are related in several ways.

Related Workplace Dilemmas

Substance abuse and AIDS are both viewed by many persons as lifestyle choices which represent conflicts between the rights of individual employees to privacy and the need of employers to maintain efficiency by reducing health care costs, reducing liability risks, and maintaining a productive work force. Both these values are important, and resolving conflicts between them requires addressing ethical dilemmas rather than merely technical solutions. That is, a rational decision-making process is rarely as appropriate as are values clarification and compromise, both within society as a whole and within each company and agency.

Related Public Policy Issues

Second, the compartmentalization of AIDS and substance abuse as separate public policy issues has meant that the solutions adopted for each issue are disastrous when the two issues are considered together. Our societal response to substance abuse has been increased law enforcement and correctional system efforts. These have not been successful at reducing the supply of or demand for illegal drugs. Our societal response to AIDS has been first to ignore the issue as a public health problem and then to panic about its dangers. This has meant that we have developed and implemented a criminal justice policy which attempts to control use of illegal drugs by arresting drug users and sellers and confining them together in increasing numbers in state and local prisons. They are incarcerated under conditions which by their very nature are conducive to homosexual activity.

Focus of Conflict: Business Responsibility or Public Health Issue?

Third, both substance abuse and AIDS are complex and costly public policy issues for society and the individual employer. Yet here it seems that the employer and society have fundamentally differing objectives, and the responsibility for addressing this conflict within the workplace falls first and foremost on the personnel director. In brief, the employer's legitimate objective is to reduce the costs of substance abuse and AIDS in the workplace by excluding as many people as possible who may be substance abusers or AIDS carriers. Personnel directors may recognize that maximizing this objective requires that employees' rights to privacy or handicap protection be violated. It may also mean increasing demands on the public health system by externalizing the costs of substance abuse and AIDS from the employer to the larger society as a whole.

Public health advocates and political leaders, on the other hand, expect employers to bear an increasing share of the costs of treating substance abuse and AIDS. They argue persuasively that employers' attempts to externalize the costs of substance abuse and AIDS to the larger society are irresponsible because our public health systems are already burdened with far more problems than they can address with available resources. And these efforts are futile because it is impossible to keep all substance abusers or AIDS victims out of the work force. Instead, what they accomplish is to further reduce the political, economic, and social power of groups whose present marginalization already contributes to a range of urban social problems.

CONFLICT BETWEEN EMPLOYER EFFICIENCY AND EMPLOYEE RIGHTS

These philosophical issues are not very important to the daily decisions personnel directors make. Human resource managers tend to design personnel systems based on short-term consequences for their employer and to measure these consequences in economic terms. On this basis, it can safely be predicted that personnel systems of the future will increasingly be characterized by greater conflict between the values of individual rights and efficiency.

Less Privacy for All Employees

In particular, all jobs will be characterized by a greater lack of privacy and a greater blurring of the distinction between work life and personal life.[1] Examples are the use of questionnaires, interviews, and preemployment physical examinations to monitor employees' behavior off the job with respect to such areas as substance abuse and sexual preferences. This is done regardless of the relationship of these behaviors to job performance.

More Concern for Liability Risk Management

The increased risk of lawsuits and the increased tendency of juries to hold employers liable for compensatory and punitive damages resulting from violations of employee and client rights has led employers to develop liability risk-management strategies for all employees. Several of these strategies have developed as a result of improved human resource management strategies: better background investigations, better orientation and training, critical-incident evaluation, and contracting out.

More efficient personnel management means better background investigations to determine whether applicants have the skills, abilities, or qualifications needed to perform a job. For example, personnel directors in major public and private employers routinely check to verify claimed education, employment, and references given by an applicant. Better background investigations allow employers to screen out applicants who may be legal or medical liability risks. Indeed, the possibility of screening out these applicants requires that the employer do so or be found negligent. For example, a hotel guest was sexually assaulted by a hotel employee. She sued the hotel and was awarded damages because the jury ruled that the employer should reasonably have known that the employee had a history of sexual assaults and should either not have hired him or not placed him in a client contact position.

Better orientation and training are a vital means of improving or updating employee skills and knowledge, particularly in fields experiencing rapid change. Yet it is also a risk-management technique. If there is ever a lawsuit alleging that an employee violated a co-worker's or customer's rights, it enables the employer to affirm that the employee was acting outside his or her official capacity and not acting in accordance with employer policy or procedures. Based on this, the employer can reduce the risk of being held liable for employee actions which violate company policy or the rights of others.

Critical-incident evaluation is a performance evaluation technique which enables the employer to provide an employee with immediate, objective, job-related feedback on job performance. When tied to progressive discipline, it is used to establish minimally acceptable levels of performance below which disciplinary action will be taken. The severity of the discipline is tied to the frequency and severity of the performance deficiency. These are also risk-management techniques because they provide for the immediate termination of employees for behavior which is so far outside the employer's personnel rules that the employee poses a grave risk to himself or others. Examples would be substance abuse for employees in critical "public welfare" or "sensitive" positions.

Contracting out is the ultimate risk-management technique. Employees are legally the responsibility of the contractor rather than the employer. Contractors must be bonded and must assume responsibility for damages arising out of their performance. Contracting out also enables the employer to manage human resources more efficiently by hiring temporary or part-time employees to adjust to workload fluctuations, rather than to overstaff to ensure that there are enough workers for peak workload periods.

THE DEVELOPMENT OF A TWO-TIER LABOR MARKET

Beyond these consequences for job design in general, there will be increasingly apparent differences between the characteristics of managerial and professional jobs in major private and public employers (first-tier labor market), and all other jobs (second-tier labor market). This bifurcated labor market is a consequence of a compromise between two valid but contradictory assumptions about the basis for organizational effectiveness: (1) Employees are more productive if they are given autonomy or shared responsibility for performing a variety of tasks which they can meaningfully relate to a significant outcome,[2] and (2) jobs are performed most efficiently if they are repetitious and routine and done by employees with minimal wages, no benefits, no employment rights, and no legal responsibility. Jobs in the first-tier and second-tier labor market can be distinguished and defined by the following characteristics.

Differential Treatment of Medically High-Risk Applicants

Applicants with specific job-related skills and abilities will be selected without reference to medical risks. This is particularly true if (1) the employer is a public agency or government contractor required to protect handicap rights of employees or applicants in the workplace, and (2) the employee is being hired into a shortage category occupation (professional, technical, or managerial).

For other positions, and particularly for jobs in the private sector, it is increasingly likely that the personnel department will use the selection process to "deselect" applicants on the basis of genetic and medical criteria, as a means of reducing personnel costs. We are progressing from a rather narrow definition of job-related physical qualifications (skills or abilities related to specific job elements) to more generalized health indicators which may indicate that the applicant is a long-term health risk.[3] An example of a narrow definition is the use of back X- rays to determine whether laborers are physically able to lift or carry, assuming these skills are required for their position. An example of a broader definition would be denying employment to employees whose general health indicators are outside normal medical limits, thereby indicating that the applicant is high-risk with respect to certain diseases or disabilities.

Our ability to predict long-term health risks by evaluating employee health profiles has been dramatically enhanced in recent years by the development of medical technology. Ironically, our interest in applying these advances to the workplace is also based on our desire to prevent the occurrence of serious health problems through health screening and employee wellness programs. But they do create the possibility that we can not only preserve the health of current employees but select out applicants whom we can reasonably predict will be greater health risks in the future.[4]

Our willingness to move in this direction is indicated by the fact that once the technology exists for genetic or medical screening, we are willing to use it as part of the selection process. Examples are: abnormal weight to height, abnormal electrocardiogram, abnormal blood chemistry (such as cholesterol levels), history of heavy drinking (as determined by liver enzyme activity), history of substance abuse (as determined by urinalysis), or likelihood of developing AIDS (as determined by AIDS antibody tests).[5]

This trend raises disturbing issues of privacy and individual rights, for future job performance or health cannot be predicted by medical tests administered as part of a preemployment physical. But it is possible to establish a statistical relationship between health indicators and the likelihood that an employee will incur serious health and life insurance benefit costs in the foreseeable future. And thus the growing need of employers and health benefit carriers to reduce costs[6] is leading them to use health indicators as one of many selection criteria.[7]

These indicators need not be determined invasively. Indeed, the two easiest methods of measuring them are through interviews and questionnaires.[8] While applicants may not respond truthfully to medical history questions or may resent them as an invasion of privacy, they may be more willing to respond to them than to undergo blood tests and urinalysis.[9] But the end result is increased emphasis on economic values (productivity and risk management) and diminished emphasis on privacy and employee or applicant rights.[10]

Increasingly, all first-tier jobs will be subject to medical risk selection criteria. Applicants will be expected to either waive any rights they may have to confidentiality of medical records or preclude themselves from being considered for employment in this labor market.

Second-tier jobs are those for which no background medical investigation is conducted. The employer elects not to screen references, verify employment history, or conduct substance abuse tests. In return, the applicant accepts the lower pay, fewer benefits, and minimal job security characteristic of these positions.

Differential Benefits

For professional and managerial employees in the first-tier labor market (major public agencies and private employers who rely on government contracts for their income), there is continued and growing recognition that benefits are a critical part of the total compensation package. These benefits include health insurance, life insurance, pension, company or agency vehicle, parking, day care, educational incentives, legal insurance, etc. These benefits constitute a significant percentage of salary. They can often be flexibly selected to match the employee's needs or to be used in combination with the benefits offered a spouse to result in a total benefit package of great value to the family unit.

Jobs in second-tier employers, or clerical and laborer jobs in first-tier employers, increasingly offer fewer benefits, if any. Usually, the employer will contract out for these services and thus pay no benefits at all. Or the employer will offer a less extensive benefit package (such as minimal group health and life insurance). Since turnover is greatest at lower-level positions, most new vacancies in the company or agency will carry a lower level of benefits.

This differential may be a deliberate policy designed to discourage employees in most positions from remaining with the company or agency for a long time. It may result from a genuine belief that the costs of not providing employer-financed benefits should legitimately be borne by employees or by public welfare systems. Examples of these beliefs are that Social Security is a substitute for employer pension systems, employees should be responsible for their own child care arrangements, and Medicare funds or private insurance should be used to provide employee medical coverage. Or it may simply be an economically-based calculation that the benefit package offered to lower-salaried or hourly employees needs to be adjusted downward if benefits are to be kept as a constant percentage of salary.

Different Motivational Models

The differential autonomy and rewards which characterize the emergent two-tier labor market are based on profoundly different motivational models. Managerial and professional positions in first-tier employers are characterized by motivational approaches emphasizing employee involvement, commitment, flexibility, and enrichment.[11] The underlying model will be one of using QWL (quality of work life) approaches so that the structure, policies, and procedures of the company or agency are open to employee involvement.[12] The objective of this approach is increased employee commitment, satisfaction, and productivity. Examples of this approach include quality circles, flexible benefit packages, teleconferencing or working at home, and flextime. In return for organizational conditions which enhance individual autonomy and self-control, the employee is expected to be productive as an individual and as a member of a work unit.[13] Managerial and professional employees in first-tier companies and agencies are offered autonomy and flexibility in exchange for diminished privacy. And this arrangement makes sense, for the blurring of the distinction between home and office means that the employer can reasonably be expected to exercise greater control over employee behavior outside the workplace.

Jobs in the second-tier labor market are designed around the opposite set of characteristics and objectives. Employees are treated as disposable commodities, to be hired when needed and released when no longer needed. Wherever possible, routine office jobs (typing, filing, phone answering, duplicating, and mailing) are eliminated by computerized word processing, computerized filing, automated phone answering systems, and fax machines.[14] Where work cannot be eliminated, it is simplified, routinized, and designed so that jobs can be performed either by machines or by people who act like machines. Positions carry minimal language, education, and skill requirements. This enables the employer to hire employees into clerical or laborer positions on a temporary, part-time, or contract basis, without worrying about the "fit" between the job and the person.[15] Examples of such positions are building and grounds maintenance, inside sales, and clerical positions.

Employees in clerical and laborer positions with first- tier employers are offered continued employment in exchange for restricted privacy. Their only option is to work for a second-tier employer offering the same privacy restrictions and a lower level of benefits and job security.

CONCLUSIONS AND RECOMMENDATIONS

These observations trace some of the interrelationships between substance abuse and AIDS as workplace issues and public policy issues. They express the author's concern that some of the natural employer responses to these issues may be based on short- term efficiency considerations. Basing employment policies solely on these considerations may lead to more severe problems in the future.

But like the Christmas Eve visions of Ebenezer Scrooge, these portents are not predictions. We can change them, if we but look at the future and decide if we like it or not. Here are some of the issues we must address in looking ahead. Since all are dilemmas rather than problems, we cannot expect to answer them absolutely. Rather, we must be content to address them constantly and clearly, making the choices that seem best under the circumstances.

Values Clarification: Privacy versus Efficiency

Substance abuse and AIDS exemplify the way contemporary public policy issues impact on society and on the workplace. They require us to confront the societal dilemma of individual privacy versus public health.[16] They also require us to confront the workplace dilemma posed by the conflict between two legitimate and opposing values—individual privacy and employer efficiency. We must decide the appropriate balance between personal privacy and medical confidentiality of employees, and health benefit cost caps and liability risk management for employers.[17]

Criminal Justice and Public Health Policy

If it has done nothing else, the AIDS epidemic has removed the cloak of invisibility that covered the conflicts between the objectives of two critical public policy areas in the United States. The objective of our criminal justice system has been to curtail use and sale of illegal drugs by prosecution and incarceration of offenders. The objective of our public health system should be to educate AIDS victims about the causes and transmission methods of the disease, to treat victims, and to prevent the spread of the disease insofar as possible.

By now it should be apparent that these policies are not working well together. On the contrary, the prison system is acting as a powerful vector for the spread of AIDS into general society. And the objectives of prisons and hospitals are basically different. We need to address ways in which these two systems, with equally legitimate objectives, can work better together.

Allocation of Jobs and Power

Jobs are the basis for individual income in the United States. They are also the basis for social, economic, and political power of the groups to which individuals belong (geographic, racial, ethnic, etc.). One of our societal values is equality of opportunity to be considered for desirable jobs (those in the first-tier labor market). Thus, there is a presumed relationship between proportional representation of all groups in the first-tier labor market, and a democratic political system.[18]

This presumed relationship between proportional representation of different groups (race, sex, ethnicity, and geography) in the first-tier labor market of a democratic political system runs counter to the emergent two-tier personnel system model that is now being developed in the interest of employer efficiency. For the two-tier model makes it less likely that individuals considered high-risk for substance abuse or AIDS will be considered for the first-tier labor market. If the two-tier system is a permanent caste system (in that persons are assigned to the first or second tier on the basis of ascribed characteristics such as race or ethnicity), then the result is a permanent division between the "haves" and the "have nots," along lines that run counter to our democratic values.

If the two-tier system is fixed but allows individuals to move from the second to the first tier on the basis of achievement (education, experience, or ability), then we must examine the mechanisms which allow individuals to do this and evaluate their adequacy. To avoid this is to engage in sophistry or hypocrisy. It means accepting a permanent caste system by default.

And regardless of whether the two-tier system allows movement for individuals from one tier to the other, we must examine the consequences of employing two contradictory motivational models and two contradictory views of human nature in the same organization. What does this do to clarity of objectives for human resource management, for clarity of communications between employers and employees, or for perceived equity of treatment between first- and second-tier employees? Do any of these contradictions undermine organizational productivity? Do they do so to a greater extent than the two-tier system enhances it?

As an alternative to the two-tier labor market, employers should look at IBM's approach—increasing productivity by providing employees with increased training and redesigned jobs. IBM has adopted a high-skill employee empowerment approach as part of its full-employment, no layoffs personnel policy. When managers at its Austin (Texas) plant estimated they could save $60 million by buying circuit boards elsewhere rather than manufacturing them, IBM had other ideas. They cut costs by upgrading worker skills, organized workers into teams, and gave teams responsibility for quality control, repairs, and materials ordering. Skill requirements for manufacturing jobs were increased, and education and training costs increased to 5 percent of payroll.

The bottom line result? Productivity is up by over 200 percent, quality is five times better, inventory has been cut 40 percent, and the plant employs more people than ever before![19]

Results such as these mean that American business would be more productive if it regarded employees at *all* levels as valuable resources rather than disposable ones. Businesses should enable employees to be more innovative and creative by providing them with jobs which involve skill and responsibility. They should provide them with the education and training needed to perform these jobs well.

Public Health Policy Objectives

Substance abuse and AIDS are public health issues because they place extraordinary demands on our public health system. And our public health system has not responded well to these pressures.[20] This system is fragmented in that there is no national policy coordination, no coordination of responsibilities between levels of government, no delineation of responsibilities among different types of providers (public, not-for-profit, and proprietary facilities), and no agreement on the appropriate roles of public health facilities and employer-financed health facilities.

And as fundamental as these disagreements are, they mask disagreement on still more basic issues and widespread public dissatisfaction with the ability of our health system to address these issues.[21] What are our national health objectives and priorities?[22] What institutional frameworks and systems will it take to accomplish these? What will it cost? Who will pay? How will the system be evaluated and regulated?

If there is a silver lining in the cloud called AIDS, it is that the demands it threatens to place on our public health system and the inability of the system as it is presently constituted to meet these demands may force public health specialists and political leaders to grapple seriously with the public policy issues it raises[23]

PERSONNEL DIRECTORS—DO THE RIGHT THING!

Personnel directors occupy a key position of responsibility in the midst of this confusion and conflict. They are the ones most responsible for developing employer policies on substance abuse and AIDS and seeing that these policies are properly implemented. To do so, they must encourage business and political leaders to clearly address the broader issues within which questions of workplace substance abuse and AIDS must be answered. They must do so with professionalism, with deference, and with an understanding that it is always easier in the short run to avoid serious issues than to address them.

But personnel directors will not succeed in developing successful workplace substance abuse and AIDS policies unless they can also work effectively as leaders to encourage society to respond to the broader issues which frame these organizational policies. They must draw upon their professionalism so that they do things right and do the right things.

NOTES

1. Kamisar, Y. (1987, September 13). Drugs, AIDS and the threat to privacy. *The New York Times Magazine, 136*, p. 108.

2. Hackman, J., & Oldham, G. (1980). *Work Redesign.* Reading, MA: Addison-Wesley, p. 90.

3. Uzych, L. (1986, Spring). Genetic testing and exclusionary practices in the workplace. *Journal of Public Health Policy*, pp. 37–57.

4. Rowe, M., Russell-Einhorn, M., & Weinstein, J. (1987, August). New issues in testing the work force: Genetic diseases. *Labor Law Journal, 38*, pp. 518–523.

5. Slater, K. (1990, June 7). Likely Methuselahs get more life-insurance breaks. *The Wall Street Journal*, pp. C1, C8; Slater, K. (1990, June 7). Blood tests used more extensively for life insurance. *The Wall Street Journal*, p. C8; and Stipp, D. (1990, July 9). Genetic testing may mark some people as undesirable to employers, ensurers. *The Wall Street Journal*, pp. B1, B3.

6. Holton. R. (1988, September). AIDS in the workplace: Underwriting update. *Best's Review, Property-Casualty Edition*, pp. 96–98; Solovy, A. (1989, January 20). Insurers, HMOs and BC-BS plans talk about AIDS. *Hospitals, 63*, p. 24.

7. Quinn, J. (1987, June 8). AIDS: Testing insurance; when science can also predict cancer and heart attacks, will anyone get health coverage? *Newsweek*, p. 55.

8. Stevens, G. (1989, Spring). Selection devices: What you see may not be what you get. *Business and Public Affairs, 15*(2), pp. 15–19.

9. Klayman, E. (1989, March). Discrimination. *Journal of Risk and Insurance, 56*, pp. 171–172.

10. McGourty, C. (1989, May 4). Human rights assessed. *Nature, 338*, p. 6.

11. Feyer, D. (1988, June). Brave new managers. *Training: The Magazine of Human Resources Development, 23*, p. 42; Lawler III, E., & Mohrman, S. (1989, April). With HR help, all managers can practice high-involvement management. *Personnel, 88*, p. 26; and Graham, E. (1990, June 4). Flexible formulas. *Workplace of the Future, The Wall Street Journal Reports*, pp. R34–R35.

12. Kafka, V. (1988, April). A new look at motivation-for-productivity. *Supervisory Management, 31*, p. 19.

13. Crossen, C. (1990, June 4). Workplace: Where we'll be. *Workplace of the Future, The Wall Street Journal Reports*, pp. R4–R8; and O'Boyle, T. (1990, June 4). From pyramid to pancake. *Workplace of the Future, The Wall Street Journal Reports*, pp. R37–R38.

14. Yoder, S. (1990, June 4). Putting it all together. *Workplace of the Future, The Wall Street Journal Reports*, pp. R24–R26.

15. Carroll, P. (1990, June 4). Computer confusion. *Workplace of the Future, The Wall Street Journal Reports*, pp. R28–R29.

16. Kleinig, J. (1990). The ethical challenge of AIDS to traditional liberal values. *AIDS & Public Policy Journal, 5*(1), pp. 42–44; Uzych, L. (1990, March). HIV testing: The legal balance between individual and societal rights. *Southern Medical Journal, 83*(3), pp. 303–307; and Doard, J. (1990, March). AIDS, stigma and privacy. *AIDS & Public Policy Journal, 5*(1), pp. 37–41.

17. Bennett, A. & Fuchsberg, G. (1990, July 2). Personnel managers meet with changes. *The Wall Street Journal*, p. B1; Working out personnel puzzles of the '90s. (1990, July 6). *The Wall Street Journal*, pp. B1, B8.

18. Mosher, F. (1982). *Democracy and the Public Service*. (Second edition). Cambridge, MA: Harvard University Press.

19. Karr, A. (1990, June 19). Workplace panel is urging changes in schools, on job. *The Wall Street Journal*, p. C15.

20. Panem, S. (1988). *The AIDS Bureaucracy*. Cambridge, MA: The Harvard University Press; and Osborn, J. (1989, Summer). Public health and the politics of AIDS prevention, living with AIDS: Part II. *Daedalus, 118*, pp. 123–144.

21. Blendon, R., Leitman, R., Morrison, I., & Donelan, K. (1990, Summer). Satisfaction with health systems in ten nations. *Health Affairs, 9*(2), pp. 185–192.

22. Anderson, R., & Miller, R. (1990, Summer). Assessing the health objectives of the nation. *Health Affairs, 9*(2), pp. 185–192.

23. Carwein, V., & Ray, C. (1989). AIDS-related income losses and implications for policy-making. *AIDS & Public Policy Journal, 4*(2), pp. 106–111.

APPENDIX A

SAMPLE SUBSTANCE ABUSE TESTING POLICY: DRUG-FREE WORKPLACE PROGRAM AND SUPPORTING POLICIES

MODEL SUBSTANCE ABUSE PROGRAM

I. Statement of Policy

(Company or agency name) acknowledges the problem of substance abuse (including alcohol) in our society. Furthermore, we see substance abuse as a serious threat to our (staff, customers, clients, and shareholders). We are addressing this problem by introducing a new substance abuse policy to ensure that the (agency or company) will have a drug-free workplace.

Drug and alcohol addiction is a complex yet treatable disease. For this reason, our substance abuse program is targeted at alleviating the problem at the commu-

---

* The following substance abuse testing policy is given solely for illustrative purposes. Employers who are contemplating the adoption of a specific policy should contact the appropriate sources of information and assistance provided in Appendix C, and their own legal counsel, prior to adoption.

nity level by involving both our employees and their families. Our commitment to eradicating substance abuse in the community reflects our firm belief that by building this community, we build our (company or agency).

While (company or agency name) understands that employees and applicants under a physician's care are required to use prescription drugs, abuse of prescribed medications will be dealt with in the same manner as the abuse of illegal substances.

The ultimate goal of this policy is to balance our respect for individual privacy with our need to keep a safe, productive, drug-free environment. Our intention is to prevent and treat substance abuse. We would like to encourage those who use drugs or abuse alcohol to seek help in overcoming their problem. In this way, fully rehabilitated abusers who remain drug-free can return to work as employees in good standing.

With these basic objectives in mind, the (company or agency) has established the following policy with regard to use, possession, or sale of alcohol and drugs.

II. Definitions

A. "Legal Drug"—includes prescribed drugs and over-the-counter drugs which have been legally obtained and are being used solely for the purpose for which they were prescribed or manufactured.
B. "Illegal Drug"—any drug: (a) which is not legally obtainable, (b) which may be legally obtainable but has not been legally obtained, or (c) which is being used in a manner or for a purpose other than as prescribed.

III. Policy and Work Rule

The (company's or agency's) policy is to employ a work force free from use of illegal drugs and abuse of alcohol, either on or off the job. Any employee determined to be in violation of this policy is subject to disciplinary action, which may include termination, even for the first offense. It is a standard of conduct of employees in the (company or agency) that employees shall not use illegal drugs or abuse alcohol. In order to maintain this standard, the (company or agency) shall establish and maintain the programs and rules set forth below.

A. General Procedures:

An employee reporting for work visibly impaired is unable to properly perform required duties and will not be allowed to work. If possible, the employee's supervisor should first seek another supervisor's opinion to confirm the employee's status. The supervisor should then consult privately with the employee to determine the cause of the observation, including whether substance abuse has occurred. If, in the opinion of the supervisor, the employee is considered impaired, the employee should be sent home or to a medical facility by taxi or other safe transportation alternative, depending on the determination of the observed impairment, accompanied by the supervisor or another employee if necessary. An impaired employee should not be allowed to drive.

B. Preemployment Drug Abuse Screening

The (company or agency) will conduct preemployment screening examinations designed to prevent hiring of individuals who use illegal drugs or individuals whose use of legal drugs indicates a potential for impaired or unsafe job performance (see "Preemployment Drug Testing Policy").

C. Current Employee Drug and Alcohol Abuse Screening

The company will maintain screening practices to identify employees who use illegal drugs or abuse alcohol, either on or off the job. It shall be a condition of continued employment for all employees to submit to drug screen:

1. When there is a reasonable suspicion to believe that an employee is using or has used illegal drugs or is abusing or has abused alcohol.

2. When there is any mishap or accident involving the employee in which injury to persons or damage to property has occurred.

3. Upon return from extended absences (see "Active Employee Drug and Alcohol Abuse Testing Policy").

D. Employee Assistance Program

The (company or agency) maintains an employee assistance program (EAP) which provides help to employees and their families who suffer from alcohol or drug abuse. However, it is the responsibility of each employee to seek assistance from the employee assistance program before alcohol and drug problems lead to disciplinary actions. Once a violation of this policy occurs, subsequently using the EAP on a voluntary basis will not necessarily lessen disciplinary action and may, in fact, have no bearing on the determination of appropriate disciplinary action.

The employee's decision to seek prior assistance from the employee assistance program will not be used as the basis for disciplinary action and will not be used against the employee in any disciplinary proceeding.

On the other hand, using the EAP will not be a defense to imposition of disciplinary action where facts providing a violation of this policy are obtained outside the EAP. Accordingly, the purposes and practices of this policy and the EAP are not in conflict but are distinctly separate in their applications.

Through the employee assistance program, the (company or agency) will provide appropriate assessment, referral to treatment, and treatment of drug and alcohol abuse (subject to the provisions of the [company's or agency's] health insurance plan). Such employees may be granted leave with a conditional return to work depending on successful completion of the agreed-upon appropriate treatment regimen, which shall include random testing.

E. Grounds for Termination or Discipline

1. Illegal Drug Use

An employee bringing onto the (company's or agency's) premises or property; having possession of; being under the influence of; possessing in the employee's body, blood, or urine in any detectable amount; or using, consuming, transferring, selling, or attempting to sell or transfer any form of illegal drug as defined above while on (company or agency) business or at any time during the hours between the beginning and ending of the employee's work day, whether on duty or not, and whether on (company or agency) business, property or not, is guilty of misconduct and is subject to discipline including discharge or suspension without pay from employment, even for the first offense. Failure to submit to required medical or physical examinations or tests is misconduct and is grounds for discharge or suspension without pay from employment.

2. Alcohol Abuse

An employee who is under the influence of alcoholic beverages at any time while on (company or agency) business or at any time during the hours between the beginning and ending of the employee's work day, whether on duty or not and whether on (company or agency) business or not, shall be guilty of misconduct and is subject to discipline including discharge or suspension without pay from employment, even for the first offense.

An employee shall be determined to be under the influence of alcohol if:

a. The employee's normal facilities are impaired due to consumption of alcohol, or

b. The employee has a blood alcohol level of .05 or higher.

Failure to submit to required medical or physical examinations or tests is misconduct and is grounds for discharge or suspension without pay from employment.

MODEL SUBSTANCE ABUSE POLICY

This (company or agency) strives to provide a safe work environment and encourages personal health. In regard to this, the (company or agency) considers the abuse of drugs or alcohol on the job to be an unsafe and counterproductive work practice.

It is, therefore, (company or agency) policy that an employee found with the presence of alcohol or illegal drugs in his/her system, in possession of, using, selling, trading, or offering for sale illegal drugs or alcohol during working hours may be subject to disciplinary action up to and including discharge. (Company- or agency-sponsored activities which may include the service of alcoholic beverages are not included in this provision).

Substance abuse includes possession, use, purchase, or sale of drugs or alcohol on (company or agency) premises, including the parking lots. It also includes reporting to work under the influence of drugs or alcohol.

An employee reporting to work visibly impaired is unable to properly perform required duties and will not be allowed to work. If possible, the supervisor should first seek another supervisor's opinion of the employee's status. Then the supervisor should consult privately with the employee with the observation, to rule out any problems that may have been caused by prescription drugs.

If, in the opinion of the supervisor, the employee is impaired, the employee should be sent home or to a medical facility by taxi or other safe transportation alternative, depending on the determination of the observed impairment, accompanied by the supervisor or another employee, if necessary. An impaired employee should not be allowed to drive.

Prescription drugs prescribed by the employee's physician may be taken during work hours. The employee should notify the supervisor if the use of properly prescribed prescription drugs will affect the employee's work performance. Abuse of prescription drugs will not be tolerated.

It is the responsibility of the (company's or agency's) supervisors to counsel with an employee whenever they see changes in performance that suggest an employee problem. The supervisor may suggest that the employee voluntarily seek help from the (company's or agency's) employee assistance program (EAP) or decide that the severity of the observed problem is such that an involuntary referral to the EAP should be made.

MODEL ACTIVE EMPLOYEE SUBSTANCE ABUSE TESTING POLICY

Employees may be required to submit to drug and/or alcohol testing at a laboratory chosen by the (company or agency) if there is a cause for reasonable suspicion of substance abuse.

Whenever possible, the supervisor should have the employee observed by a second supervisor or manager before requiring testing. Employees who refuse substance testing under these circumstances will be terminated.

Circumstances that could be indicators of a substance abuse problem and considered reasonable suspicion are:

1. Observed alcohol or drug abuse during work hours on (company or agency) premises.
2. Apparent physical state of impairment.
3. Incoherent mental state.
4. Marked changes in personal behavior that are otherwise unexplainable.
5. Deteriorating work performance that is not attributable to other factors.
6. Accidents or other actions that provide reasonable cause to believe the employee may be under the influence.

If the test results are positive, the employee may be referred to the employee assistance program (EAP). If the employee refuses treatment, or does not comply with the treatment recommended by the EAP, termination will result.

If the tests are positive and if an employee is granted a leave of absence for substance abuse rehabilitation, he or she will be required to participate in all recommended after-care and work rehabilitation programs. Upon successful completion of all or part of these required programs the employee may be released to resume work but must agree to random substance abuse testing and close performance monitoring to ensure that he or she remains drug-free.

MODEL PREEMPLOYMENT DRUG TESTING POLICY

All job applicants at this (company or agency) will undergo screening for the presence of illegal drugs or alcohol as a condition of employment.

Applicants will be required to voluntarily submit to a urinalysis test at a laboratory chosen by the company and by signing a consent agreement will release the (company or agency) from liability.

Any applicant who tests positive on an initial test shall be retested using a confirmatory test before results are used as the basis for a hiring decision.

Any applicant with positive test results will be denied employment at that time but may initiate another inquiry with the (company or agency) after six months.

The (company or agency) will not discriminate against applicants for employment because of past abuse of drugs or alcohol. It is the current abuse of drugs or alcohol which prevents employees from properly performing their jobs that the (company or agency) will not tolerate.

CERTIFICATE OF AGREEMENT

I do hereby certify that I have received and read the (company or agency name) policy and have had the Drug-Free Workplace Program explained to me. I understand that if my performance indicates it is necessary, I will submit to a drug test. I also understand that failure to comply with a drug testing request or a positive result will lead to termination of employment.

Name (please print) _____

Signature _____

Date _____

[This certificate of agreement becomes part of the active employee's personnel file.]

MODEL EMPLOYEE ASSISTANCE PROGRAM POLICY

The management of this (company or agency) is aware that many personal or health problems can and do interfere with an employee's ability to perform on the job. These problems may include emotional and mental illnesses, family and marital stress, abuse of alcohol or drugs, and many others.

Employees whose job performance problems are not related to a lack of skill and who do not respond satisfactorily to the usual disciplinary procedures are usually in need of the attention of professionals. With proper treatment, many troubled employees can be restored to a satisfactory level of job performance. However, if the underlying problems or illnesses are ignored, they may worsen with time, eventually rendering the person unemployable.

To help avoid this waste of human resources, the (company or agency) offers an employee assistance program (EAP) for the employees and their dependents as part of its employment services. The EAP provides confidential assessment, referral, and short-term counseling at no cost to employees whose personal health problems are interfering with their job performance.

If an EAP referral to a provider outside the EAP is necessary, costs may be covered by the employee's medical insurance benefit, but the cost of such outside services is the employee's responsibility.

Confidentiality is assured. No information regarding the nature of the personal problem will be made available to supervisors, nor will it be included in the permanent personnel file.

Participation in the EAP will not affect an employee's future career advancement or employment, nor will it protect an employee from disciplinary action if substandard job performance continues. The EAP is a process used in conjunction with discipline, not a substitute for discipline.

An employee can participate in the EAP through self-referral or a referral by a supervisor. In a self-referral the employee contacts the EAP counselor directly. The employee is assured that no one in the (company or agency) will be notified.

It is the responsibility of the (company's or agency's) supervisors to appropriately confront an employee whenever they see changes in performance that suggest an employee problem. The supervisor may suggest that the employee voluntarily seek help (informal referral) from the EAP or decide that the severity of the observed problem is such that an involuntary referral to the EAP should be made (formal referral).

A. Informal Referral

Informal referrals can take place at any time in the disciplinary process or if an employee confides in the supervisor that he/she is having personal problems. In an informal referral:

1. The supervisor should inform the employee of the benefits provided by the EAP and give the employee the name of the counselor and the telephone number.
2. The supervisor should contact the EAP counselor and inform him/her of the informal referral and the circumstances leading to it, but this is not strictly necessary.

In an informal referral the EAP counselor will not tell the supervisor whether the employee used the EAP and will not divulge any information to the supervisor about the visit.

B. Formal Referral

A formal referral can take place at any time during the disciplinary procedure. Through a formal referral, the supervisor directs the employee to make use of the EAP. Failure to use the EAP may result in disciplinary action up to and including termination.

In a formal referral:

1. The supervisor (or another manager designated by the company or agency) should contact the EAP counselor to discuss the employee's problem.

2. The EAP counselor will ask the employee to sign a waiver allowing the counselor to call the supervisor and tell him/her whether the employee saw the counselor and followed recommendations. No other detailed information is revealed to the supervisor.

In extreme circumstances where termination can occur the supervisor may opt to give the employee another opportunity to improve his/her performance by a formal referral to the EAP. In these cases the employee may be asked to sign an acknowledgment letter indicating that failure to go to the EAP and follow recommendations will result in termination.

Supervisors should not attempt to diagnose the nature of the employee's problem. However, they should be alert to changes in behavior that may signal a problem, such as:

- absenteeism
- chronic lateness
- personality change
- decline in work quality
- unusual behavior

AN OPEN LETTER TO THE EMPLOYEES OF (COMPANY OR AGENCY NAME)

We have come to recognize that substance abuse is a problem on the job for all of us, as well as a social problem. We believe abuse of alcohol and use of illegal drugs endangers the health and safety of the abusers and all of the others around them.

We have committed (company or agency name) to creating and maintaining a drug-free workplace without jeopardizing valued but troubled employees' job security, providing they are prepared to help us help them.

Our policy now formally states that substance abuse will not be tolerated during working hours or on the premises of (company or agency name), including the parking lots. This prohibition includes the possession, use, or sale of illegal drugs or alcohol. (Company- or agency-sponsored activities which may include the service of alcoholic beverages are not included in this provision.)

Employees who are found to be under the influence of illegal drugs or alcohol or who violate this policy in other ways are subject to disciplinary action, which may include termination. Because of the serious nature of these violations, each individual case will be thoroughly investigated to determine the appropriate course of action.

In order to assist us in maintaining a safe and healthful workplace, we have created an Employee Assistance Program (EAP). The EAP provides employees and their families confidential assessment, short-term counseling, referral and follow-up for personal or health problems, including emotional and mental illness, family and marital stress, alcohol, and drug abuse, among others.

This service provides three counseling sessions, at no cost to the employee or the employee's family, with further medical referrals covered by medical insurance when appropriate.

The (company or agency name) has contracted with a private concern, (EAP provider name), to provide these services at no charge to you, your spouse, or your children. Immediate help can be obtained by calling (EAP provider name) at (phone number).

An employee can contact the EAP directly or can be referred by a supervisor. Every communication with the EAP which is initiated by the employee is confidential, and the (company or agency) will not be notified.

Employees who suspect they have personal problems should call the Employee Assistance Program (EAP). The EAP can help the employee overcome the problem before it has an adverse effect on his or her employment situation.

Referrals to the EAP may also be made by supervisors of the (company or agency) where personal problems are suspected to be the cause of job performance deficiencies. The EAP can also assist supervisors in formulating a strategy for handling employees whom they suspect have a drug, alcohol, or other personal problem.

It is important that all of us work together to deal with substance abuse and other personal problems to make the (company or agency) a safer and even more rewarding place to work.

Sincerely,

Chief Executive Officer

APPENDIX B

SAMPLE WORKPLACE AIDS POLICY

Purpose: The purpose of this policy is to inform employees about AIDS (Acquired Immune Deficiency Syndrome), and to explain how this (company or agency) is responding to this health issue.[1]

Responsibility: The personnel department of (company or agency name) will be responsible for directing and coordinating the development and implementation of this policy. The major elements of this policy are infection control (health care employers only), education of employees, counseling and referral services for AIDS victims, and protection of their handicap rights. Assistance from other departments

---

* This model policy was compiled through a number of sources, including: Myers, P., & Myers, D. (1987, April). AIDS: Tackling a tough problem through policy. *Personnel Administrator, 32/*(4), pp. 95–107, 143; and AMA Membership Publication Division (1988). *AIDS, The New Workplace Issues* (New York: Academy of Management); and *Guidelines on AIDS and first aid in the workplace, WHO AIDS Series 7* (1988). Geneva: World Health Organization. It is given solely for illustrative purposes. Employers who are contemplating the adoption of a specific policy should contact the appropriate sources of information and assistance provided in Appendix C, and their own legal counsel, prior to adoption.

and the EAP (employee assistance program) is also required. Their specific responsibilities will be described below.

INFECTION CONTROL (Health Care Employers Only)[2]

1. To protect the health and safety of employees and patients, all employees will be required to undergo orientation and training in universal precautions (infection control policies and procedures). These policies and procedures will include:
   - body substance precaution
   - needle stick
   - mandatory reporting and evaluation of exposures
2. Employees who feel they may have been exposed to AIDS on the job are required to report the incident immediately.
3. If they so request, these employees will be tested for AIDS.
4. If they test positive, they will be removed from positions involving the risk of blood-to-blood contact with patients and other employees.
5. Employees who are AIDS-positive will not be restricted from work duties except as noted in (5) above, provided that it is determined in consultation with the employer's medical director and the employee's physician that:
   - The employee is free from any other infection or illness for which restriction is indicated
   - The employee is not at risk of being susceptible to infections he or she might come in contact with in the line of work.

EDUCATION

All current and new employees and supervisors will receive education training emphasizing the following points:

1. AIDS cannot be transmitted or contracted in the workplace. AIDS is a fatal illness which cannot be transmitted or contracted through routine workplace contact. Nor can it be transmitted through any other means except sexual relations, intravenous drug use, a transfusion from infected blood, or from an infected mother to her child.
2. AIDS victims are legally entitled to handicap protection.
   - AIDS is a handicap. Employees with AIDS are entitled to retain their jobs provided they can, with reasonable accommodation, perform them satisfactorily.
   - It is illegal to discriminate against temployees on the basis of their being AIDS carriers. Harassment of AIDS victims by co-workers or supervisors is not only illegal, but subjects the employer to punitive damages for allowing discrimination against handicapped persons to occur.
   - Employees and supervisors will be disciplined if they harass co-workers who have AIDS.

3. Co-workers of AIDS employees will not be transferred or reassigned.
   - Because AIDS is not transmittable from employees to co-workers or clients in the workplace, and because isolation or discipline of AIDS victims is a violation of their handicap rights, requests for transfer or reassignment of co-workers of AIDS victims who fear that they will be infected will not be granted. Management's refusal to grant such requests will not be considered grievable under any collective bargaining agreement to which (company or agency) is a party.
   - Employees who refuse to work with co-workers who have AIDS will be subject to disciplinary action for insubordination or job abandonment.
   - Employees who harass co-workers known or suspected to have AIDS will be subject to disciplinary action, including termination.
   - Supervisors who have reasonable cause to know that harassment of known or suspected AIDS victims is occurring, and do not take steps to prevent it, will be subject to disciplinary action including termination.
4. The (company or agency name) provides many economic benefits to AIDS victims and their survivors. (Include any of the following which are available)
   - light-duty positions
   - disability retirement
   - employee health and life insurance benefits
   - employer-financed health and life insurance benefits which may extend beyond the period of active employment
   - retirement, life insurance, and Social Security benefits to which survivors of the employee are entitled.
5. Medical Records are Confidential.
   - AIDS is a medical condition which does not affect most victims' ability to perform their jobs.
   - Employee medical records will be kept confidential, with one exception. In the event that the employee voluntarily requests reasonable accommodation in order to remain on the payroll, the employee will be required to advise the immediate supervisor and the personnel director of this request (so that reasonable accommodation strategies may be implemented).
   - Other release of the information (such as to co-workers, other supervisors, or union officials) for any reason whatsoever is a violation of (company or agency) policy. Employees or supervisors who release or use this information will be subject to disciplinary action, including termination.
6. Voluntary disclosure enables AIDS victims to get better treatment and hold their jobs longer.
   - Prompt detection and treatment of AIDS can extend the life of the victim, perhaps indefinitely.
   - AIDS victims can remain employed longer and better provide for survivors if they voluntarily disclose their condition.
7. Employees who have AIDS but do not disclose this condition to the (company or agency) will not be eligible for handicap protections.

- The (company or agency) cannot be expected to make reasonable accommodation for the needs of AIDS victims unless they request such accommodation by voluntarily disclosing their condition.
- Such employees who are unable to perform their required job duties will be subject to disciplinary action, including termination.

8. Employees will not be subject to mandatory AIDS testing.
   - AIDS is not transmittable from employees to other employees or clients in the workplace.
   - Workplace AIDS testing of applicants or employees is not a cost-efficient or effective means of detecting AIDS carriers or stopping the spread of the disease.
   - Workplace AIDS testing is a violation of employees' right to reasonable expectation of privacy.

9. AIDS victims deserve compassion, not punishment.
   - AIDS is a disease caused by a virus. The disease is painful, debilitating, and fatal.
   - AIDS may be transmitted as a result of practices resulting from lifestyle choices (anal intercourse by male homosexuals or needle sharing by intravenous drug users); or it may be transmitted unknowingly to infants, to the heterosexual partners of bisexual males or intravenous drug users, or to transfusion recipients.
   - Blaming AIDS victims for the disease is an irrational defensive reaction caused by other employees' unjustified fears of catching AIDS in the workplace.

10. The employer's AIDS policies and procedures will be public information. Patients, employees, health and life insurance carriers, and outside accrediting bodies will be advised of the workplace AIDS policies and procedures that the (company or agency) has adopted.

COUNSELING AND REFERRAL SERVICES

The (company or agency) will have an EAP (employee assistance program), whose responsibilities include counseling and referral services for employees who have AIDS and for their immediate family members. It will be the function of the EAP to:

- Clarify employer policies to employees who have AIDS or fear they may have it, with respect to such topics as handicap protection, reasonable accommodation, available benefits, and confidentiality of medical records.
- Refer the employee to counseling and support groups in the community (see Appendix C), or to health care providers for appropriate services covered under the (company or agency) health benefits policies.
- Keep counseling and referral services strictly confidential, except that the employee's immediate supervisor and the personnel director must be notified if the

employee requests reasonable accommodation. If the employee who has AIDS does not wish to divulge this to his or her supervisor, the EAP will respect the employee's privacy. It will then be up to the supervisor to initiate disciplinary action if and when the employee can no longer perform the duties of the position without reasonable accommodation.

HANDICAP PROTECTION

The (company or agency name) recognizes that AIDS is considered a handicap under federal and state employment discrimination laws. Therefore:

- AIDS victims are legally entitled to handicap protection. It is therefore illegal to discriminate against applicants or employees in any personnel action on the basis of their being AIDS carriers.
- Employees with AIDS are entitled to retain their jobs provided they can, with reasonable accommodation, perform them satisfactorily.
- Even if they cannot perform their current jobs satisfactorily with reasonable accommodation, AIDS victims are entitled to "light-duty" positions, if any are available, as an alternative to being removed from the workplace once their leave is exhausted.
- Harassment of AIDS victims by co-workers or supervisors is illegal and a violation of (company or agency) policy. Employees who harass co-workers known or suspected to be AIDS victims, or supervisors who might reasonably be expected to know that this harassment is occurring but allow it to continue, will be subject to disciplinary action including termination.

NOTES

1. The employer may wish to develop a specific AIDS-related policy, or to develop a general policy covering AIDS and other life-threatening diseases. This model policy is written for AIDS; the wording should be changed appropriately if it is to cover other illnesses as well.

2. Bows, R. (1989, December). Medical and legal ramification of transmission of HIV to hospital employees. *American Journal of Hospital Pharmacology*, *46*, 12 Supp. 3, pp. S3-4; and Banta, W. (1988). *AIDS in the workplace* (Lexington, MA: D.C. Health & Co.).

APPENDIX C

WHERE TO GET HELP WHEN YOU NEED IT

SUBSTANCE ABUSE TESTING POLICIES AND PROGRAMS

Federal Agencies

U. S. Office of Personnel Management
1900 E Street, NW
Washington D.C. 20415

State Governments (including local agencies under their jurisdiction)

Alabama:
Division of Alcoholism and Drug Abuse
Department of Mental Health
135 S. Union
Montgomery
Alabama 36130

Alaska:
  Office of Drug Abuse
  Department of Health and Social Services
  Pouch H-05F
  Juneau
  Alaska 99811

Arizona:
  Drug Abuse Programs
  Division of Behavioral Health Services
  Department of Health Services
  2500 East Van Buren
  Phoenix
  Arizona 85008

Arkansas:
  Office of Drug and Alcohol Abuse Prevention
  Department of Social & Rehabilitative Services
  1515 Building
  1515 West 7th
  Little Rock
  Arkansas 72203

California:
  California Department of Alcohol & Drug Abuse
  111 Capital Mall
  Sacramento
  California 95814

Colorado:
  Alcohol and Drug Abuse Division
  Department of Health
  4210 East 11th Avenue
  Denver
  Colorado 80220

Connecticut:
  Connecticut Alcohol and Drug Council
  Department of Mental Health
  90 Washington Street
  Hartford
  Connecticut 06115

Delaware:
  Bureau of Substance Abuse
  1901 North DuPont Highway

New Castle
Delaware 19720

Florida:
Bureau of Drug Abuse Prevention
Division of Mental Health
Department of Health & Rehabilitative Services
1317 Winewood Boulevard
Tallahassee
Florida 32301

Georgia:
Alcohol and Drug Abuse Section
Division of Mental Health & Retardation
Department of Human Resources
618 Ponce De Leon Avenue, N.E.
Atlanta
Georgia 30308

Hawaii:
Alcohol and Drug Abuse Branch
Department of Health
1270 Queen Emma Street, Room 404
Honolulu
Hawaii 96813

Idaho:
Bureau of Substance Abuse
Division of Community Rehabilitation
Department of Health and Welfare
700 West State Street
Boise
Idaho 83720

Illinois:
Dangerous Drugs Commission
300 North State Street, 15th Floor
Chicago
Illinois 60610

Indiana:
Division of Addiction Services
Department of Mental Health
5 Indiana Square
Indianapolis
Indiana 46204

Iowa:
  Iowa Drug Abuse Authority
  505 5th Avenue
  Des Moines
  Iowa 50319

Kansas:
  Drug Abuse Unit
  Department of Social & Rehabilitative Services
  Biddle Building
  2700 West 6th Street
  Topeka
  Kansas 66608

Kentucky:
  Alcohol and Drug Abuse Branch
  Division for Prevention Services
  Bureau of Health Services
  Department of Human Resources
  275 East Main Street
  Frankfort
  Kentucky 40601

Louisiana:
  Bureau of Substance Abuse
  Division of Hospitals
  Louisiana Health & Human Resources Admin.
  200 Lafayette Street
  Baton Rouge
  Louisiana 70804

Maine:
  Office of Alcoholism and Drug Abuse Prevention
  Bureau of Rehabilitation
  32 Winthrop Street
  Augusta
  Maine 04330

Maryland:
  Drug Abuse Administration
  Department of Health & Mental Hygiene
  Herbert O'Conor Office Building
  201 West Preston Street
  Baltimore Maryland 21201

Massachusetts:
 Division of Drug Rehabilitation
 Department of Mental Health
 160 North Washington Street
 Boston
 Massachusetts 02114

Michigan:
 Office of Substance Abuse Services
 3500 North Logan Street
 P.O. Box 30035
 Lansing
 Michigan 48909

Minnesota:
 Drug and Alcohol Authority
 Chemical Dependency Division
 Department of Public Welfare
 658 North Cedar Street
 St. Paul
 Minnesota 55155

Mississippi:
 Division of Drug Misuse
 Department of Mental Health
 619 Lee State Office Building
 Jackson
 Mississippi 39201

Missouri:
 Division of Alcoholism & Drug Abuse
 Department of Mental Health
 2002 Missouri Boulevard
 Jefferson City
 Missouri 65101

Montana:
 Addictive Diseases Division
 Department of Institutions
 1539 11th Avenue
 Helena
 Montana 59601

Nebraska:
 Nebraska Commmission on Drugs
 P.O. Box 94726
 State Capitol Building

Lincoln
Nebraska 68509

Nevada:
Bureau of Alcohol and Drug Abuse
Rehabilitation Division
Department of Human Resources
505 East King Street
Carson City
Nevada 89710

New Hampshire:
Office of Drug Abuse Prevention
3 Capital Street, Room 405
Concord
New Hampshire 03301

New Jersey:
Division of Narcotic & Drug Abuse Control
Department of Health
129 East Hanover Street
Trenton
New Jersey 08625

New Mexico:
Drug Abuse Agency
Department of Hospitals and Institutions
P.O. Box 968
Santa Fe
New Mexico 87503

New York:
Office of Drug Abuse Services
Executive Park South
Albany
New York 12203

North Carolina:
North Carolina Drug Commission
325 North Salisbury Street
Raleigh
North Carolina 27611

Ohio:
Ohio Bureau of Drug Abuse
Division of Mental Health Department of Mental Health
and Mental Retardation

65 South Front Street
Columbus
Ohio 43215

Oklahoma:
Division of Drug Abuse Services
Department of Mental Health
P.O. Box 53277, Capitol Station
Oklahoma City
Oklahoma 73105

Oregon:
Programs for Alcohol and Drug Problems
Mental Health Division
Department of Human Resources
2575 Bittern Street, N.E.
Salem
Oregon 97310

Pennsylvania:
Governor's Council on Drug & Alcohol Abuse
Riverside Office Center
Building No. 1, Suite N
2101 North Front Street
Harrisburg
Pennsylvania 17110

Rhode Island:
Rhode Island Drug Abuse Program
Department of Mental Health and Retardation and Hospitals
303 General Hospital
Rhode Island Medical Center
Cranston
Rhode Island 02920

South Carolina:
South Carolina Commission on Alcohol and Drug Abuse
3700 Forest Drive
P.O. Box 4616
Columbia
South Carolina 29240

South Dakota:
Division of Drugs and Substance Control
Department of Health
Joe Foss Building

Pierre
South Dakota 57501

Tennessee:

Alcohol and Drug Abuse Section
Department of Mental Health
501 Union Street, 4th Floor
Nashville
Tennessee 37219

Texas:

Drug Abuse Division
Department of Community Affairs
Box 13166, Capitol Station
Austin
Texas 78711

Utah:

Division of Alcoholism and Drugs
150 North Temple
Salt Lake City
Utah 84110

Vermont:

Alcohol and Drug Abuse Division
Department of Social & Rehabilitative Services
State Office Building
Montpelier
Vermont 05602

Virginia:

Department of Mental Health/Mental Retardation
Division of Substance Abuse Control
Commonwealth of Virginia
P.O. Box 1797
Richmond
Virginia 23214

Washington:

Office of Drug Abuse Prevention
Community Services Division
DSHS, OB-43E
Olympia
Washington 98504

West Virginia:

Division of Alcoholism and Drug Abuse
Department of Mental Health

1800 Kanawha Boulevard, East
Charleston
West Virginia 25305

Wisconsin:
Bureau of Alcohol & Other Drug Abuse
Division of Mental Hygiene
Department of Health and Social Services
One West Wilson Street, Room 523
Madison
Wisconsin 53702

Wyoming:
Drug Abuse Programs
Hathaway Building, Room 457
Cheyenne
Wyoming 82001

Private Sector Employers

American Management Association
135 West 50th Street
New York
New York 10020
212/903-8070

Labor Unions

Community Action Program
AFSCME (American Federation of State, County and Municipal Employees)
1625 L Street, NW
Washington, D.C. 20036
202/429-1215

Professional Associations and Clearinghouses

Alcohol and Drug Problems Association of North America
444 North Capitol Street, NW
Washington, D.C. 20001
202/737-4340

American Council for Drug Education
204 Monroe Street, Suite 110
Rockville

174

Maryland 20850
301/294-0600

American Society for Public Administration
1120 G Street, NW
Washington D.C. 20005
202/393-7878

Association of Labor-Management Administrators and Consultants
1800 North Kent Street, Suite 907
Alexandria
Virginia 22209
703/522-6272

Clearinghouse on Workplace Drug and AIDS Policy
Department of Public Administration
Florida International University
North Miami
FL 33181
305/940-5987

EAP Marketplace Directory
2145 Crooks Road
Suite 103
Troy
Michigan 48084
313/643-9580

Employee Assistance Society of North America
P.O. Box 3909
Oak Park
Illinois 60303
312/383-6668

International Commission for Prevention of Alcoholism and Drug Dependency
6830 Laurel Street, NW
Washington
D.C. 20012
202/722-6730

National Committee for Prevention of Alcohol and Drug Dependency
RR 1, Box 635
Appomattox

Virginia 24522
804/352-8100

International Personnel Management Association
1617 Duke Street
Alexandria
Virginia 22314

National Clearinghouse for Alcohol Information
1776 East Jefferson, South 4th Floor
Rockville
Maryland 20857

National Clearinghouse for Mental Health Information
Office of Communications and Public Affairs
5600 Fishers Lane, Room 11A-33
Rockville
Maryland 20857

National Council on Alcoholism
12 W. 21st Street, 7th Floor
New York
New York 10010
212/206-6770

National Safety Council
Labor Department
444 N. Michigan Avenue
Chicago
Illinois 60611
312/527-4800

National Drug Abuse Center for Training and Resource Development (for drug abuse professional training materials)
5530 Wisconsin Avenue
Washington
D.C. 20015

Prevention Branch
Division of Resource Development
National Institute on Drug Abuse (for guidance on the development of prevention programs)
5600 Fishers Lane, Room 10A-30

Rockville
Maryland 20857

U.S. Drug Enforcement Administration
Information Systems Section
Drug Abuse Warning Network
1405 Eye Street, NW
Washington
D.C. 220537
202/633-1316

U.S. Public Health Service
National Clearinghouse for Drug Abuse Information
Parklawn Building, Rm. 10A-43
5600 Fishers Lane
Rockville
Maryland 20857
301/443-6500

800/COCAINE
Toll-free information referral hotline for drug abusers. Sponsored by the national
Psychiatric Institutes, Based at Fair Oaks Hospital in Summit, New Jersey.

800/843-4971
Toll-free hotline for employers trying to clean up drug abuse. Sponsored by the
National Institute on Drug Abuse in Rockville, Maryland.

213/825-3736
Computer bulletin board with up-to-date information on drug abuse bibliogra-
phies, consultants, organizations, videotapes, and films for uses of IBM-com-
patible microcomputers. Based at the University of California at Los Angeles.

AIDS TESTING POLICIES AND PROGRAMS

Public Agencies

U.S. Department of Health & Human Services
Public Health Service
Centers for Disease Control
National AIDS Information Clearinghouse
P.O. Box 6003
Rockville
Maryland 20850
   HOTLINE: 800/342-2437 (recorded message)
   COUNSELOR: 800/342-7514

Professional Associations and Clearinghouses

AIDS Action Council
2033 M Street, NW
Washington D.C. 20036
202/293-2886
   (national lobbying organization which represents 700 community-based organizations providing services to people with AIDS)

AIDS Coalition to Unleash Power (ACT UP)
496A Hudson Street, Suite G4
New York New York 10014
212/989-1114 (and other local chapters)
   (political action and information network among local AIDS-activist organizations)

American Association of Physicians for Human Rights (AAPHR)
2940 16th Street, #105
San Francisco CA 94103
415/255-4547
   (national clearinghouse and referral service for physicians and medical students concerned about human rights issues, including treatment of persons with AIDS)

American Foundation of AIDS Research (AmFAR)
5900 Wilshire Boulevard
2nd Floor, East Satellite
Los Angeles
CA 90036
213/857-5900

1515 Broadway
Suite 3601
New York
New York 10036
212/719-0033
   (leading private-sector funding organization in the United States dedicated to AIDS research, education, and public policy)

The American Red Cross
1730 D Street, NW
Washington
D.C. 20006
202/737-8300 (and other local chapters)
   (provides AIDS-related education and training materials for use in schools and

the workplace, plus provides support services to persons with AIDS and their families)

American Social Health Association
National STD Hotline 800/227-8922

Computerized AIDS Education Network (CAIN)
Gay and Lesbian Community Service Center
1213 North Highland Avenue
Los Angeles
California 90038
213/854-3006
   (funded by the State of California, this computerized database provides information to subscribers twenty-four hours per day; listings are free)

Mothers of AIDS Patients
P.O. Box 3152
San Diego
California 92103
619/544-0430
   (provides information and emotional support to persons with AIDS and their families)

The Names Project
P.O. Box 14573
2362 Market Street
San Francisco
California 94114
415/863-5511
   (sponsors the AIDS Memorial Quilt and raises money to provide services for persons with AIDS and their families)

National AIDS Network
2033 M Street, Suite 800
Washington
D.C. 20036
202/293-2437
   (community-based network of AIDS organizations; provides technical assistance grants and referral services to member organizations)

National Association of People With AIDS
2025 Eye Street, NW
Suite 1118
Washington

D.C. 20005
202/429-2856
> (association of local organizations by and for persons with AIDS; provides information and referrals to persons with AIDS and advocates for their rights)

National Council of Churches
AIDS Task Force
475 Riverside Drive, Room 572
New York
New York 10115
202/870-2421
> (preventive education and a resource and information packet for use by religious leaders in their congregations)

National Gay Task Force AIDS Hotline
800/221-7044

National Leadership Coalition on AIDS
1150 17th Street, NW, Suite 202
Washington
D.C. 20036
202/429-0930
> (consolidates support in response to AIDS by over 170 corporate, labor, and civic organizations)

TELEPHONE LISTINGS FOR LOCAL AND STATE ORGANIZATIONS

This listing is drawn from a more extensive directory compiled by the National AIDS Network. Contact this organization directly if you need help and your community is not listed below. If two numbers are given for an organization, the first is a general office number and the second a hotline number offering AIDS information, referrals, and sometimes counseling services. All 800 numbers are hotlines, as are most local numbers ending in 2437 (AIDS).

Alabama

Birmingham: AIDS Outreach, 205/322-0757, 322-4197
Mobile: AIDS Support System, 205/433-6277
Montomery: AIDS Outreach, 205/284-2273

Alaska

Anchorage: Alaska AIDS Project, 907/276-4880, 800/248-AIDS

Arizona

Phoenix: Arizona AIDS Project, 602/420-9396
Tucson: AIDS Project, 602/322-6226, 800/248-AIDS

Arkansas

Little Rock: Arkansas AIDS Foundation, 501/663-7833, 800/448-8305

California

Bakersfield: AIDS Hotline, 800/448-8305
Berkeley: Gay Men's Health Collective, 415/644-0425
Fresno: Central Valley AIDS Team, 209/264-2437
Los Angeles: AIDS Project, 213/876-AIDS, 800/922-AIDS, 213/962-1600; Minority AIDS Project, 213/936-4949
Riverside: Inland AIDS Project, 714/784-2437
Sacramento: AIDS Foundation, 916/448-2437
San Diego: AIDS Project, 619/543-0300, 619/543-0604
San Francisco: AIDS Foundation, 415/864-4376
San Luis Obispo: AIDS Task Force, 805/549-5540
Santa Barbara: Tri-Counties AIDS Project, 805/681-5120
Santa Rosa: Sonoma County AIDS Project, 707/576-4734

Colorado

Boulder: Boulder County AIDS Project, 303/444-6121
Denver: Colorado AIDS Project, 303/837-0166

Connecticut

Hartford: Gay/Lesbian Health Collective, 203/236-4431
New Haven: AIDS Project, 203/624-2437

Delaware

Wilmington: Delaware Lesbian and Gay Health Advocates AIDS Cooperative, 302/652-6776

District of Columbia

Whitman Walker Clinic/AIDS Program, 202/332-5295, 202/797-3562

Florida

Statewide: 800/FLA-AIDS
Ft. Lauderdale: AIDS Center One, 305/485-7175
Key West: AIDS Help, Inc., 305/296-6196
Miami: Health Crisis Network, 305/326-8833, 800/443-5046, 305/634-4636
Orlando: Central Florida AIDS Unified Resources, Inc., 407/849-1452
Tampa: AIDS Network, 813/221-6420

Georgia

Athens: AIDS Athens, 404/542-2437
Atlanta: AID Atlanta, 404/872-0600, 800/551-2728, Outreach, Inc., 404/873-5992
Macon: Central City AIDS Network, 912/742-2437
Savannah: First City Network, Inc., 912/236-CITY

Hawaii

Honolulu: Life Foundation, 808/971-2437

Idaho

Boise: Idaho AIDS Foundation, 208/345-2277

Illinois

Champaign: Gay Community AIDS Project, 217/351-AIDS
Chicago: AIDS Comprehensive Center, 312/908-9191, AIDS Foundation, 312/642-5454

Indiana

Evansville: AIDS Resource Group, 812/423-7791
Fort Wayne: AIDS Task Force, 219/424-0844
Indianapolis: APIC Indiana AIDS Task Force, 317/634-1441, 317/257-HOPE

Iowa

Des Moines: Central Iowa AIDS Project, 800/445-AIDS

Kansas

Topeka: AIDS Project, 913/232-3100
Wichita: AIDS Referral Services, 316/264-2437

Kentucky

Lexington: AIDS Crisis Taskforce, 606/281-5151
Louisville: Community Health Trust of Kentucky, 502/636-3341, 502/454-6699

Louisiana

Baton Rouge: AIDS Task Force, 504/923-2277
New Orleans: NO/AIDS Task Force, 504/891-3732, 800/992-4379

Maine

Bangor: Eastern Maine AIDS Network, 207/990-3626
Portland: AIDS Project, 207/774-6877, 775-1267, 800/851-AIDS

Maryland

Baltimore: Health Education & Resource Organization (HERO), 301/685-1180,
800/638-AIDS
Rockville: Montgomery County HERO, 301/762-3385

Massachussetts

Boston: AIDS Action, 617/437-6200, 800/235-2331

Michigan

Detroit: Michigan AIDS Hotline/AIDS Wellness Networks, 313/547-9040, 800/
872-2437
Grand Rapids: AIDS Task Force, 616/459-9177

Minnesota

Minneapolis: Minnesota AIDS Project, 612/870-7773, 800/248-AIDS

Mississippi

Jackson: Mississippi Gay Alliance, 601/353-7611

Missouri

Columbia: Mid Missouri AIDS Project, 314/875-2437
Kansas City: Good Samaritan Project, 816/561-8784; Free Clinic, 816/231-
8895, 231-8896
St. Louis: Effort for AIDS, 314/531-2847, 314/531-7400

Montana

Billings: AIDS Support Network: 406/252-1212

Nebraska

Omaha: Nebraska AIDS Project, 402/342-4233, 800/782-AIDS

Nevada

Las Vegas: Aid for AIDS of Nevada, 702/369-6162; Gay Switchboard of Las Vegas, 702/733-9990
Reno: Nevada AIDS Foundation, 702/329-2437

New Hampshire

Manchester: New Hampshire AIDS Foundation 603/595-0218

New Jersey

New Brunswick: AIDS Education Project, 201/763-0668; Hyacinth Foundation, 201/246-8439, 800/433-0254
Newark: New Jersey Lesbian & Gay AIDS Awarness, 201/763-2919; St. Michaels, 201/877-5524

New Mexico

Albuquerque: New Mexico AIDS Services, 505/266-0911
Las Cruces: SW AIDS Committee, 505/525-AIDS

New York

Albany: AIDS Council, 518/434-4686, 518/445-AIDS
Bronx: Pediatric AIDS Hotline, 212/430-4227, 212/430-3333
Brooklyn: AIDS Task Force C.S.P., 718/596-4781, 718/638-AIDS
Buffalo: Western New York AIDS Program, 716/847-2441, 716/847-AIDS
Huntington Station: Long Island Association for AIDS Care, 516/385-2451, 516/385-AIDS
New York: Bailey House AIDS Resource Center, 212/206-1001; Gay Men's Health Crisis, 212/807-6664, 212/807-6655; Health Resources Administration, 212/645-7070; Minority Task Force on AIDS, 212/749-1214; National Gay Task Force AIDS Hotline, 212/807-6016
Richmond Hill: AIDS Center of Queens County, Inc., 718/896-2500
Rochester: AIDS Rochester, Inc., 716/232-3580, 716/232-4430

Syracuse: AIDS Task Force of Central New York, 315/475-2430, 315/875-AIDS
White Plains: Mid-Hudson Valley AIDS Task Force, 914/993-0606, 914/993-0607

North Carolina

Asheville: Western N.C. AIDS Project, 704/252-7489
Charlotte: Metrolina AIDS Project, 704/333-1435, 704/333-2437
Durham: Lesbian & Gay Health Project, 919-683-2182
Greensboro: Triad Health Project, 919/275-1854
Raleigh: AIDS Control Progam, 919/733-7301
Wilmington: Grow AIDS Resource Project, 919/675-9222
Winston-Salem: AIDS Task Force, 919-723-5031

Ohio

Akron: AIDS Task Force, 216/375-2960
Canton: AIDS Task Force, 216-489-3231
Cincinatti: Ambrose Clement Health Clinic, 513/352-3139
Cleveland: Health Issues Task Force, 216/621-0766
Columbus: AIDS Task Force, 614/488-2437, 800/332-2437

Oklahoma

Oklahoma City: Oasis Community Center, 405/525-AIDS
Tulsa: Shanti Tulsa, 918-749-7898

Oregon

Eugene: Willamette AIDS Council, 503/345-7089; AIDS Prevention for Youth, 503/342-2782
Portland: Cascade AIDS Project, 503/223-5907, 800/777-AIDS; Oregon AIDS Task Force, 503/226-6678

Pennsylvania

Harrisburg: So. Central AIDS Assistance Network, 717/238-AIDS
Philadelphia: Action AIDS, 215-981-0088; AIDS Task Force, 215/545-8686, 215/732-AIDS
Pittsburgh: AIDS Task Force, 412/363-6500, 412/363-2437, 800/282-AIDS

Rhode Island

Providence: Project AIDS, 401/831-5522, 800/726-3010

South Carolina

Columbia: Carolina AIDS Research and Education, 803/777-2273
Palmetto AIDS Life Support Services, 803/779-7257, 800/868-PALS

South Dakota

Sioux Falls: Sioux Empire Gay and Lesbian Coalition, 605/332-4599

Tennessee

Chattanooga: Chattanooga Cares, 615/265-2273, 615/757-2745
Knoxville: AIDS Response, 615/523-AIDS
Memphis: Aid to End AIDS Committee, 901-458-AIDS, AIDS Coalition, 901/726-1690
Nashville: Nashville Cares, 615/385-1510, 615/385-AIDS

Texas

Austin: AIDS Services, 512/472-2273
Corpus Christi: Coastal Bend AIDS Foundation, 512/883-5815, 512/883-2273
Dallas: AIDS Resource Center, 214/521-5124, 214/559-AIDS
El Paso: SW AIDS Committee, 915/533-6809, 915/533-2437
Houston: AIDS Foundation, 713/623-6796, 713/524-2437; Community AIDS Prevention Project, 713/439-0210
San Antonio: Tavern Guild AIDS Fund, 512/821-6218

Vermont

Burlington: Vermont Cares, 802/863-2437

Virginia

Charlottesville: AIDS Support Group, 804/979-7714
Norfolk: Tidewater AIDS Crisis Taskforce, 804/423-5859
Richmond: AIDS Information Network, 804/355-4428, 804/355-AIDS

Washington

Lacey: Olympia AIDS Task Force, 206/352-2375
Seattle: Northwest AIDS Foundation, 206/329-6923

Wisconsin

Madison: Madison AIDS Support Network, 608/255-1711
Milwaukee: AIDS Project, 414/273-2437, 800/334-2437

Index

About the Authors

DONALD KLINGNER is Director of the Clearinghouse on Drug and AIDS Testing and Professor of Public Administration at the School of Public Affairs and Services, Florida International University.

NANCY G. O'NEILL is a Research Associate with the Clearinghouse on Drug and AIDS Testing.